# Spells
## and How They Work

*By the same authors*

Eight Sabbats for Witches
The Witches' Way
The Witches' Goddess
The Witches' God
The Life and Times of a Modern Witch

# Spells
## and How They Work

Janet and Stewart Farrar

With line illustrations by Stewart Farrar

PHOENIX PUBLISHING INC.

PHOENIX PUBLISHING INC.
Portal Way
P.O. Box 10
Custer, Washington USA 98240


ISBN 0-919345-63-8

Cover design by Rick Testa

Printed in the U.S.A.


By printing this book on recycled paper we have saved:

- 68 mature trees
- 28,000 gallons of water
- the energy equivalent to heat and air condition an average American
  home for 2 years
- 240 pounds of pollutants from being released into the atmosphere
- 12 cubic yards of waste that would ordinarily end up in a landfill

# Contents

# *Illustrations*

PICTURE CREDITS

Alan Meek: 1–2. Stewart Farrar: 3–9.

# *Figures*

To Barbara, Peter and Rhiannon Lee-Doyle
*Beannacht Bhandé libh*

# Introduction

Entitling a book *Spells and How They Work* may seem to be begging the question by assuming from the start that they do. So let us make our own position clear.

It is our experience, as practising witches for twenty years, that provided they are properly performed, with an understanding of the principles involved – yes, spells do work; if not always, then at least far more often than either coincidence or alternative explanations would allow.

Given this attitude, it is only sensible to ask oneself (1) why they work; (2) what are the operational principles used in making them work; (3) what code of ethics should one observe in deciding whether, and how, to perform a spell; and (4) what are the dangers involved.

In this book, we have tried to answer all these questions and a good many others. We have also given many examples of spells old and new.

But we would like to make one thing emphatically clear from the start. Observing the code of ethics (which we deal with in Chapter III) is not just a matter of being virtuous and able to live with your conscience. Unethical spell-working is not only harmful to the 'target'. It is also extremely dangerous, and in the end self-destructive, to the person who works them. Not in any hypothetical Hell, but here and now.

To end with a personal plea. Our earlier books have provoked a steady flood of readers' letters which still continues by almost every post; and we take this opportunity of apologizing to those readers to whom, through sheer pressure of work, we have replied inadequately or not at all. Many of them have asked us to work spells for them. Please do not ask it this time. Trying to solve the problems of dozens of strangers whom we have never met would drain us, or anyone else, in a week. It would also be irresponsible, because, however honest the writer tries to be, one cannot have the whole picture; after all, what doctor would diagnose and prescribe by post? And if you read this book carefully, we hope you will find we have pointed a way towards solving such problems for yourself.

Janet Farrar
Yule, 1989                                                       Stewart Farrar

# I  *Do Spells Work?*

The materialism of the Scientific and Industrial Revolutions of the past couple of centuries has dismissed as fantasy, or as purely psychological phenomena, all manifestations of psychic abilities and power; though, under it all, folklore and grass-roots instinct have known better. In recent years, the atmosphere has changed; serious scientists are investigating psychic phenomena on the assumption that there is something to investigate. And witches, and many others (including Christian faith-healers), are actively putting psychic powers to practical use. Much of this activity can be classified as 'spells', even though some of the activists would shun the word – and there is overwhelming evidence that, properly done, spells do work.

The rationalism of recent centuries has achieved much. It has enabled us to master the physical level of reality to a degree undreamed-of before. It has made life (in some countries at least) healthier, longer, safer and better provided-for; anyone who thinks otherwise, and could time-travel back to slave-based Rome, or

Inquisitorial Spain, or Victorian London or Dublin, within a week would rush back to our epoch as fast as he could press the button.

But the very enthusiasm and single-mindedness of that rationalism has thrown out some important babies with the bathwater. One of the most vital of these is the understanding that matter is not the only level of reality; that the other levels (which we shall examine in the next chapter) are not mere superstition but active areas with laws of their own which can be understood with sufficient application.

The rationalist revolution has come full circle. It has brought us to frontiers within science itself at which the laws of mechanical materialism are no longer adequate; which is why the frontiersmen of that science are rethinking their vision of reality.

This book is about spells. Till recently, our rationalist culture lumped them with the other 'superstitions' it believed it had outgrown. But a 'spell' is merely a deliberate process for achieving a desired aim; what differentiates it from other such processes is that it uses levels and laws which mechanical materialism disowned. (It is interesting that the rationalist culture, with its gift for compartmentalization, has accepted prayer as at least respectable; yet what is prayer but a form of spell, an attempt to achieve what you want by putting yourself in tune with the non-material levels of reality?)

To work a spell, one must not dismiss rationality; one must use it as a tool, to understand the laws of the levels involved, to plan the operation in accordance with those laws, to analyse the results honestly and to learn from experience both the fruitful methods of working and the pitfalls one may encounter. And the paradox of this is that one must learn, rationally, when it is necessary to put rationality on one side and to work by intuition, emotion and all the faculties which rationality prefers to tame. And (again rationally) one must know the right moment to switch back.

Because in our experience, and countless other people's, spells are not superstition. They are an effective method of achieving legitimate aims.

Let us look, then, at some of the laws and principles involved.

# II  *Why and How*

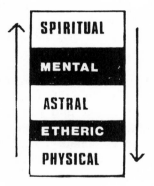

If effective spell-working depends on 'levels of reality' and on understanding their laws and their interaction, what are those levels?

The names generally given to them in occult philosophy are the spiritual, mental, astral, etheric and physical levels – some of them often subdivided. They are relevant, of course, both to the cosmos as a whole and to ourselves as human individuals. Since spell-working is an activity of human individuals, we will consider the levels particularly in that context.

UPPER SPIRITUAL  This is the level of pure or abstract spirit, the inner divine spark of each of us. It draws its energy directly from the Great Unmanifest, the ultimate source of all things. Its astrological symbol is the Sun.

LOWER SPIRITUAL  Sometimes known as concrete spirit. Occult theory holds that each of us is of the nature of one of the seven rays of the spectrum of existence, and that it is at the lower spiritual level that our particular ray sets the keynote of our individuality. Its astrological symbol is Jupiter.

UPPER MENTAL    Abstract mind, where the individual starts to form concepts under the influence of one's spiritual nature. Its astrological symbol is Mercury.

LOWER MENTAL    Concrete mind, defining, analysing and categorizing concepts and accumulating memory. Its astrological symbol is Saturn.

UPPER ASTRAL    Abstract emotions. Urge to relatedness. Images and thought-forms relevant to this. Its astrological symbol is Venus.

LOWER ASTRAL    Instincts and passions. Urge to attract or possess. Images and thought-forms relevant to this. Its astrological symbol is Mars.

ETHERIC    The tenuous energy-web of near-matter which links all the above levels with the physical, thus maintaining it in being. Its astrological symbol is the Moon.

PHYSICAL    Dense matter, the material body. Its astrological symbol is the Earth.

In reincarnation theory, it is held that the spiritual and upper mental levels of a human being constitute the Individuality, the immortal part which survives from life to life and which contains both male and female essences in balance; while the lower mental, astral, etheric and physical levels form the Personality, the transient 'suit of clothes' which the individuality acquires for each separate incarnation and which is sometimes male, sometimes female.

As the astral level is of particular importance in spell-working, the above definition should be amplified a little. The division into upper and lower astral is something of an over-simplification; experience shows that the astral plane is a continuous spectrum. At its upper end, its images and thought-forms are near-mental but belong on the astral because they are infused with emotion. At its lower end, it is sometimes called the astral counterpart of physical manifestation, in that each physical entity or object is closely associated with an astral image of itself; obviously, it is the astral counterpart of a given object or person that spell-working seeks to influence, through imagination (an astral function), concentration (mental) and willpower (something of both), as a direct path to influencing the physical.

The important thing to remember about these levels is that they speak and understand different languages. The mental level uses words and logical processes. The astral and physical levels both work in the language of the Unconscious; the astral level in symbols and images, the physical level in sensations – tactile, somatic, visual and so on. So successful spell-working must involve effective communication between them all, the mental level using logical planning to achieve this before the working starts, not during it.

As Andraste of San Francisco puts it:

> Sensual involvement in the working and its attributes is of prime importance in raising energy. The unconscious self is the only gateway to the higher self, and involving the Unconscious means utilizing senses, symbols, feelings and ritual, not rationality and logic.

This principle of 'different languages' for the various levels is important to grasp. For many people, it is the stumbling-block which makes them categorize spell-working as superstition and mumbo-jumbo. For example, in our list above we have given the astrological symbols of the various levels – Mercury for the upper mental, Saturn for the lower mental, and so on. And the correspondences, you will find, include such things as Tarot cards, mythical beasts and pagan deities.

The point is that one does not even have to accept the effect of Venus and Mercury in trine, or the promises of the Nine of Pentacles, or the baleful warnings of the Basilisk, or the existence of Ishtar, to realize that they are useful symbols for relationship, categories, attitudes and qualities. And the more we learn of their traditional meanings, the subtler and more complex a communication-system we can build up between the levels.

After all, the most firmly rationalist of us use metaphors in everyday speech – 'sticky wicket', 'on another tack', 'minding our p's and q's', 'a cross to bear' – not because we are cricketers, sailors, printers or Christians but because they convey precise meanings in encapsulated form. So why should we not use (for example) the symbol of Jupiter to express productive organization, even if we have doubts about astrology?

The Unconscious wants, and needs, to communicate with the Ego-consciousness (and vice versa) for the health and efficiency of the total entity. It cannot communicate in words, so it will grasp eagerly any symbols which the Ego-consciousness understands and offers it, and will add these symbols to its vocabulary of communication.

Spell-working depends on understanding, and deliberately using, the laws of interaction between the levels. So if that involves building up such vocabularies of 'irrational' symbols, is not that a rational step to take? We may even find, in the process, that some of these symbols are not quite so 'irrational' as we once thought.

# III  *The Ethics of Spell-Working*

The ethics of spell-working are not just pious thoughts to be paid lip-service to, like the admirable morality of a Sunday sermon which is shelved in practical weekday life. They are a set of principles the ignoring of which can and will have disastrous consequences, and not only for the person at whom the spell is aimed; such damage is very often transient anyway, if the person is psychically and emotionally healthy. Ignoring them can (and if persisted in, certainly will) do lasting harm to the spell-worker.

Selfish, malignant or irresponsible spell-working in the end bounces back on the spell-worker; we shall consider this 'Boomerang Effect' in the next chapter. But it is also a slippery slope, a self-infection which does cumulative harm to the personality.

The ethical motto of spell-working must be the Wiccan saying: 'An it harm none, do what thou wilt' – and 'do what thou wilt' does not mean 'anything goes'; it means 'have your legitimate aim clearly in mind, and work to achieve it'. The emphasis should be on the 'do' rather than on the 'wilt'.

The rules can be summed up as follows:

1. Never work to harm anyone.
2. Never work to manipulate anyone against his or her own will or natural development.
3. Never assume you know all the factors involved in the situation or person you are working on.
4. Never work for your own gain at someone else's expense.
5. Word your spell precisely and carefully, to leave no loopholes which may result in your inadvertently breaking Rules 1 to 4.

Rule 1 is self-explanatory. Consider even a well-intentioned spell honestly and unhypocritically, and you will know if it breaks it.

Rule 2, again, calls for self-examination even when you think your spell is well-intentioned. It is all too easy to persuade yourself (like a possessive parent) that you know what is best for the person concerned.

Susa Morgan Black of San Francisco puts it well: 'When you create something, you will have to deal with the results. Anything you "put out there" will come back at you. Love magic, for instance, to entice the wonderful Mr Aloof. We are all on our own individual paths, and have free will. To toy with someone else's free will is disastrous. It may seem to work for a while, but the price is self-destruction. Whenever I do a spell, I add the clause "and may this spell work for the greatest good of all", or "an it harm none".'

Elen J. Williams of London warns:

> We should be wary of doing good' to people whether they want it or not! It is very easy, and comforting to coven members and those asking for working, to work at a rather low and superficial level. I think that a high ethical stance demands that we really think and *feel* through what we are doing, even when things look on the face of it to be 'obviously beneficial'.
>
> This raises the question as to whether we should ever work for someone without their knowledge. I don't think we should make any hard and fast rule about this; we sometimes do so, but we always consider the ethics of it first very carefully indeed, and realize that we have to take complete responsibility for what we do.

Wicca Française (a well-organized federation of covens in France and some other countries) tell us: 'We never put out any curses, but we may influence some of our members and their friends, when they have an exam to pass (driving tests or what have you), so as to facilitate things for them. But the beneficiaries are themselves informed, and are often the first to put the request to us.'

Not everyone would be as rigid as this about informing the person worked for. We find, for example, that there are sometimes cases when help is obviously needed and can be given – but the person concerned, however friendly on a personal basis, might be nervous at the thought of witchcraft being worked for them! But whatever the reason, spell-working without informing must be very carefully considered before-hand to decide if it is justified.

One often beneficial result of a person's knowing that he or she is being worked for is what we call the Placebo Effect (with which every doctor is familiar). Often we have been asked for spell-working, especially for healing, and have promised to give it – intending, say, to work for it at our next coven Circle. Then, before we have even been able to do it, the person has got in touch to thank us for its success – the problem is solved, the condition cured or whatever. In fact, the mere knowledge that the work is being done has had the necessary effect on the person concerned, and thus on the situation or condition. Well and good; but one should never rely on the Placebo Effect or take advantage of it. In fact, it is a sound practice to reaffirm and strengthen the success magically as soon as one can.

Rule 3 is well expressed in the Sioux Indian prayer: 'O Great Spirit, let me not judge my neighbour till I have walked a mile in his moccasins.' Here, too, one is apt to assume on inadequate information that one knows what is best for a person or a situation. Do your homework very thoroughly before taking action.

This underlines what we said in the Introduction: that, even with the best of intentions, working spells for strangers whom you have not met face-to-face, but who have merely written asking for help, is fraught with pitfalls. If the problem seems serious enough, get the applicant to come and see you, and even then proceed cautiously; or put someone reliable who lives near the applicant in touch with him or her.

Rule 4, too, calls for thought. There is nothing immoral about spell-working for your own needs or even for your reasonable desires in excess of basic needs; but you must be sure no one else will suffer if it succeeds. To take an extreme example: working for needed money is very practical – but do you really want it to come by Uncle Fred's dying young and leaving it to you in his will? Here, too – careful wording, and 'an it harm none'.

We shall go into the implications of Rule 5 – precise formulation – in Chapter VI, where we deal with the actual steps involved in preparing and working a spell.

Basically, ethical spell-working is concerned with fruitfulness, pro-gress, health, problem-solving and the removal of barriers. Unethical spell-working is concerned with power-seeking, regardless of the consequences – which can become as addictive as hard drugs and just as self-destructive.

'The seeking for power,' Tezra from California points out, 'is not in itself an evil pursuit; but many who have sought power have sought it in evil places, and also in sources easily drained. I prefer a source so great that it can never be drained, and only grows greater by sharing. I prefer to see us as lenses for focussing the power, and the Power is both out there, in the Earth, and in each of us. Each person takes what she or he needs, and grounds or releases the rest; and being so great, and renewable, there is a lot left over.'

Ethical spell-working, and an understanding of what Starhawk calls the distinction between 'power-over' and 'power-from-within', is not just morally praiseworthy. It is also one hell of a lot safer.

# IV  *The Boomerang Effect*

The Boomerang Effect is expressed in the traditional occult maxim: 'Any psychic attack which comes up against a stronger defence rebounds threefold on the attacker.'

'Threefold' may sound rather more metaphorical than precise – how would you measure the rebound? – but taking it to mean 'with even greater effect', we have certainly found it to be true; and it is one of the greatest practical (in addition to the ethical) reasons for refraining from malevolent magic. Morality apart, not even the most powerful black magician can be sure that he will never encounter that stronger defence; which is why black magic is always, in the end, self-destructive.

'A stronger defence' can mean three things. First, of course, conscious and deliberate defence when you are aware of the attack. Second, the habit of keeping yourself permanently in a state of defence. And third, a naturally tough psychic skin – which many people, even without any occult knowledge or even a belief in psychism, do possess.

A balance should always be kept between the first and second aspects. A round-the-clock obsession with psychic defence can amount to paranoia and divert energy and attention from positive matters. The best attitude to develop is one of calm confidence and of improving your psychic awareness, so that you will always know pretty quickly if an attack is on the way. The improving of psychic awareness and sensitivity is a central aim of Craft practice – and it should be seen as an all-round development, for sensitivity to positive phenomena and opportunities and to the needs of others, not merely to threats.

We shall go into the subject of psychic self-defence in the next chapter, but we will emphasize here that the answer to psychic attack should never be counter-attack, which is fraught with danger; it should be reliance on the Boomerang Effect by strengthening your own defences and, if necessary, a binding spell, which we explain in Chapter XIX.

Valerie Worth (*The Crone's Book of Words*, p. 98) gives a spell for breaking a curse so that it returns to its source. You collect four fallen twigs – one each of hazel, oak, elm and willow – and hold them in the smoke of a fire while you repeat seven times:

> Turner be turned,
> Burner be burned:
> Let only good
> Come of this wood.

You then spit on each twig, break it small and throw them in the fire. 'The curse will die with the fire's death.'

After so much discussion of principles, this is the first spell we have quoted which involves what the rationalist would call 'mumbo-jumbo'. Why the four twigs, why specifically those four trees and why the spitting and the burning?

We shall be quoting dozens more of such spells, particularly in Chapters XI–XIV. The formulae, actions and objects or substances they involve may have many different purposes. Sometimes they may be, frankly, just to impress the uninitiated. Sometimes they may be a distorted memory of something which originally had a physically, psychologically or psychically practical reason. And even oftener they may be calling upon a symbolism, whether conscious or unconscious, which aids the inter-level communication we spoke of on pp. 16–17.

What one should not do is to dismiss them out of hand just because the reason for their form is not immediately obvious to rational analysis. You may find that they work though you don't know why – that the power of their symbology is buried too deeply in your personal Unconscious (or even in the Collective Unconscious) for your conscious awareness to find it.

A traditional spell is often rather like poetry, in that the power can manifest even though the reasons for its working remain a mystery.

It is best to keep a cautiously open mind.

Susa Morgan Black sends us another way of ensuring the Boomerang Effect and deflecting bad energy back to the sender, the symbology of which is more apparent.

'Take a special hand-held mirror,' she says, 'and simply turn completely around with the mirror reflecting outward and state an affirmation like –

> 'Circle of Reflection,
> Circle of Protection,
> May the sender of all harm
> Feel the power of this charm.'

We have used mirrors for this purpose ourselves when we have known who was working against us, and in what direction he or she lived. We would put a mirror in a suitable window facing outwards in that direction, willing it to send the malevolence back to its source.

But such working really leads us into the next chapter.

# V  *Psychic Self-Defence*

'The only thing to fear is fear itself' (a condensation of F.D. Roosevelt's memorable declaration) is often cited in occult teaching. It contains an important truth but, like many nutshell truths, it is an over-simplification.

Fear in the sense of the three p's – paranoia, panic and paralysis – is entirely negative, undermining our defences. Fear in the sense of awareness of danger, stimulating preparedness to deal with it and causing the adrenalin to flow, is the natural security system of any species, including our own.

When it comes to spell-working, awareness of the Boomerang Effect is, as we have seen, the most confidence-inspiring element in that security system. That effect, though, depends upon a healthy defence; and there are many things one can do about this.

The primary, round-the-clock defence is an attitude of calm confidence, the knowledge that your own working is positive and non-malignant, so that there are no chinks in your psychic armour on that score.

But there are times when either trained instinct or factual information tells you that extra, short-term defence is advisable.

The basic defence of this kind is the Magic Circle.

The witches' Circle has, in fact, two functions: protective and amplifying. It keeps out unwanted influences, and it prevents the power that is built up from dissipating until the moment for its purposeful release. Both these are specified in the ritual statement made while casting the Circle.

We have given the Circle-casting and banishing rituals in full in our earlier books (see Bibliography). We would merely re-emphasize here that the working should always be done within a Circle, even if it is only a mentally 'zipped-up' one; and that the zipped-up Circle is a useful conditioned reflex to develop for a time when attack is known or suspected.

By a zipped-up Circle we mean quickly but vividly envisaging a protective Circle around yourself, cast deosil. And remember that 'Circle' really means a sphere or ovoid, completely enclosing you. It should be envisaged as a faintly glowing violet egg through which no harm can pass, and its reality on the astral plane should be confidently accepted.

It should also be seen as moving with you and still enclosing and protecting you as you move about, even inside a speeding vehicle.

Its astral quality is not self-delusion – it is the truth. Our coven Maiden, Ginny, who lives three miles away from us, is very psychically sensitive and says she can always tell when we have cast a Circle round our bed at night. It is something we (not being paranoid) seldom feel the need to do; but time and again, when Ginny has told us we have done it, she has been right.

Valerie Worth (*The Crone's Book of Words*, p. 15) sums up the relative importance of physical aids and mental attitude very neatly:

> Hang an ash-bough
> Over your door,
> Fill your pockets
> With iron nails,
> Carry always
> The mullein-leaf,
> But say these words
> Against the worst:
>
> *I stand*
> *In circles*
> *Of light*
> *That nothing*
> *May cross.*

Talking of Circles round the bed – when you are casting a protective Circle at home, you should always consider how big you should make it. An attack turned back by such a Circle may well expend itself on someone nearby but outside it; so be ready to cast one round the whole house if there is someone else in it who might be vulnerable. Such protection should also be extended to animals, who are extremely sensitive and vulnerable.

(We shall refer on p. 90 to the medieval belief that witches kept animal familiars which were not what they seemed, but disguised demons. In fact, if they were not mere pets, they would have been very much what they seemed – real animals, kept precisely because real animals have a useful sensitivity. They can warn you, by their uneasy behaviour, when there is something psychically 'not quite right' about the atmosphere, or about a particular place, before you become aware of it yourself. Our own experience, and other people's, has often borne this out.)

A Circle once cast, it should be banished (dispersed) when its purpose is over, or reinforced by recasting if it is to continue.

When the direction from which an attack is coming is known, an effective reaction is the Banishing Pentagram of Earth gestured in that direction with your right forefinger (or purely mentally, if someone is watching and you want your action to remain private). This is done by tracing the five-pointed star round all its sides, starting from the bottom left to the apex and tracing the others in sequence (see Fig. 1).

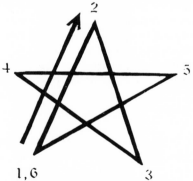

Fig. 1 – Banishing pentagram

If the actual direction is not known but the attacker is, he or she should be envisaged as standing before you. If you know both the direction and the attacker, so much the better.

The physical or envisaged action should, of course, be accompanied by a vigorous mental rejection of the attack – but not with any wish for harm to the attacker. If he or she experiences the Boomerang Effect as a result, that is his or her responsibility; but harm as such should never be willed.

This is particularly important (in addition to the ethics of the matter) because psychic attack is rarely direct or even deliberate. It may stem from bottled resentment (in which case, ask yourself honestly if you have justified it – and if you realize that you have, taken steps to put it right; the simple word 'Sorry' is a powerful spell in itself) or from someone's paranoia about a situation or class of people which just happens to include you (in which case the culprit is to be pitied and healed, not attacked). Or it may be a case of vampirism.

Vampirism, in sensible occult terminology, has nothing to do with the horror-film image. It refers to people who drain others' vital energy. This can be done deliberately, by knowledgeable 'black' occultists, but this kind of vampirism is far rarer than some people think.

Some individuals are pathological vampires, drawing energy unhealthily off others which they should be drawing healthily from the universal Source and from its manifestation in surrounding Nature. One can and should protect oneself against such people – and since they vary widely in degree, such protection can range from simply taking them in small doses (we all have friends in that category!) to active and determined psychic defence of the kinds we are describing in this chapter.

Pathological vampires, like alcoholics, need curing, not condemning. Whether you are prepared or equipped to attempt such a cure is up to you, but it is not really a subject for this book.

Vampirism may also be temporary, as a by-product of illness or personal crisis, and such cases need handling with compassion and understanding. Elderly invalids can be particularly prone to it, and young children in the same house particularly vulnerable to them; so if such a situation exists, look discreetly to the protection of the children.

Suspected psychic attack may actually be nothing of the kind, but a situation of astral turbulence, connected, for example, with a crisis of political or community tension. If such turbulence is diagnosed, the best defence is to isolate yourself from the turbulence – refusing, for example, to be drawn into fruitless arguments. This does not mean, of course, disowning your responsibilities as a citizen or withdrawing into an ivory tower. It means keeping calm and assessing the situation from within your psychic armour. It is the tension you isolate yourself from, not the problem itself.

All this may seem a digression from the subject of psychic defence against malignant spell-working. But, in fact, the symptoms which make one suspect psychic attack can have a number of different causes, and it is extremely important to know about them, and to learn to distinguish between them, before leaping into defensive action.

That said, let us get back to the practical side of psychic defence.

Protecting a whole house or flat can be done in various ways more long-lasting than a Circle. One way is to consecrate water and salt and to sprinkle the mixture round the whole perimeter, marking a Banishing Pentagram at each opening – door, window, chimney, ventilation grating and so on. Another is to place a small mirror in each window, facing outwards.

(Traditional formulae for consecrating water and salt are brief, so perhaps they should be repeated here. That for water is: 'I exorcise thee, O Creature of Water, that thou cast out from thee all the impurities and uncleanness of the spirits of the world of phantasm, in the names of — and —.' And for salt: 'Blessings be upon this Creature of Salt; let all malignity and hindrance be cast forth thencefrom, and let all good enter therein. Wherefore I bless thee and invoke thee, in the names of — and —.' These consecrations are done either with the point of an athame or merely holding up the bowl in both hands. The salt is then poured into the water.)

Returning for a moment to psychic attack which is based on paranoia. The situation may arise (all too often in occult circles, unfortunately) when an individual or group becomes convinced that you are acting against him, her or them and starts reacting accordingly. This can often be more of a nuisance than a danger, and if reasoned confrontation fails, one or more of the standard forms of defence should be enough. If the attack persists, it will often simply burn itself out – or if (again, unfortunately too frequently in occult circles) it has become the subject of gossip but one keeps one's cool about it, the sources are very likely to end up by making a laughing-stock of themselves.

One active form of defence against such attack, if it does persist, is to earth it. For example, take a piece of iron, consecrate it and will it to become a conductor for the malign influence. Then bury it outside your home with just the tip showing, so that it can attract the influence into itself and pass it into the earth to disperse.

Mother Earth is more than capable of taking any such charge of energy, neutralizing its malignancy and re-using the energy itself fruitfully. But if you are at all uneasy about this – for example, if there are vulnerable plants nearby – also consecrate a ring of copper wire a foot or so across, as an isolator of the malignancy, and bury it to surround the iron but before the iron is inserted. You can now regard that patch of soil as your psychic compost heap. (With a little imagination, you will find that this iron-spike spell can be adapted to other useful purposes.)

It should not be necessary to underline, by now, that all such symbolic or ritual gestures – in fact, all the defence procedures mentioned in this chapter – are useless without strong visualization of their purpose, and equally strong determination that the purpose shall be achieved.

We have dealt with rituals of protection on a wider basis than spell-working in *The Witches' Way*, Chapter IX; and for a deeper study of the subject as a whole, we recommend Dion Fortune's *Psychic Self-Defence* and Murry Hope's *Practical Techniques of Psychic Self-Defence*.

# VI  *Setting About It*

A spell can be as simple or as complicated as the occasion demands. But be it simple or complex, three factors are essential: precise visualization of intent, concentration and will-power.

Concentration and willpower speak for themselves. Concentration is an ability built up by practice, and some find it easier than others. Will-power includes confidence – and that depends largely on an understanding of the various levels of reality and their interaction, and the sure knowledge that they exist. Given that understanding and knowledge, it is much easier to have confidence that, if you have done it properly, your spell will work. And that in turn makes it easier to apply your will-power.

Both concentration and will-power contribute to the building-up of magical power – the psychic charge, whether of an individual or of a group, which must be brought to the maximum possible intensity and then discharged to achieve the intended purpose.

Visualization, however, is not so simple and requires careful consideration. It involves two aspects: first, the very precise definition of the aim to be worked for; and second, the clear visualization of whatever symbols or images need to be borne in mind to achieve that aim.

The aim itself should be expressed in words before you start – and in words as exact as a solicitor's document designed to leave no room for possible misunderstanding or loopholes. Very little experience with spell-working will teach you that sloppy or metaphorical wording leads time and again to unexpected, and sometimes unwanted, results; we shall consider some cases of this in Chapter X.

The very first step, then, is to formulate (and, in the case of group working, to agree upon) the aim to be worked for, very clearly indeed. This is absolutely essential to success and to the avoidance of 'misfires'.

Elen J. Williams puts it well:

> We often spend quite a lot of time in a meeting talking about the work we are about to do, and tuning in to the problem. We will then start getting a clear idea of how we should work, what forces we are up against, and which we should ally ourselves with. For example, one member asked us to work for the return of a loan. Instead of working on the money or the borrower, it became suddenly clear that we should work to strengthen the lender's power to ask for his rights in a way that would brook no further procrastination.
>
> Similarly, when discussing healing work for someone, we have occasionally had a clear idea that it was not our job to do that – almost as if it would be interfering in the private business of that person who had their own path to tread through their illness, perhaps to death. In these situations, we work to give that person our love and support, and to strengthen the beneficent spiritual forces around them.
>
> Essentially we try to work with the harmonizing and creative natural forces, recognizing that these often look destructive in the short run. Our most successful work has been when the forces have been well aligned and clearly understood. This is easiest when we know the person really well, and some of our most successful work has been to do with the spiritual and psychological growth of coven members.

Christine Best of Tralee points out that a problem which seems, at first glance, to involve negative action can usually be reassessed and tackled in a positive way. Her coven knew a couple who had split up, and each had a new partner; but the woman of the original couple was causing trouble – for example, trying to turn the children against their new stepmother – not because she wanted them or the man back but out of spite. The coven's first instinct was to bind and restrain her; but on more careful consideration, they decided to work for the woman's peace of mind and happiness in her new relationship (which she had, after all, chosen herself). This worked, and overall harmony was restored.

The multi-level principle we discussed in Chapter II is not just a theory in the background; it must be an attitude of mind. Andraste of San Francisco tells us:

> I find in general that an awareness of levels is important. Once the awareness that a spell is needed or could be helpful enters the mind, and the mind begins to plan how to work the spell, one shortly gets to the level of visualization, symbols, correspondences, and involvement of physical links in the actual working.
>
> The manipulation of the object-links then moves the energy through the archetypal and mental levels, and if it is released, it is free to affect the physical world.
>
> Letting go of a spell's energy is extremely important in allowing the energy the freedom to work.

Or as Susa Morgan Black summed it up for us: 'A key element in magic is "LET GO".'

Discharging the psychic energy raised is important in all magical working, and particularly in spell-working. We have witnessed cases in which this has been overlooked – and the result has been not only frustration of the intent but, on the physical level, a severe headache for the practitioner!

Susa stresses the importance of a literally childlike frame of mind during spell-working: 'In their minds, children can make anything happen; and sometimes, what the children play at, actually manifests itself in their life. This has happened to me many, many times .... Little by little we are discouraged and belittled out of that state of mind, in order to Grow Up. I feel that magic is a return to that wondrous state of "anything can happen", and that frame of mind is the one we seek to create magic. The closer we can come to that mindset, the more effective our rituals and spells become.'

A spell must never become routine, or genuine concentration will be impossible – even for children. A prayer is a spell too, of course, since it involves clear visualization of a desired aim, plus the conscious effort to tap the ubiquitous source of power, however one names it. But any sensible Christian would admit that daily prayers can easily become mere repetitive formulae, automatic and lifeless. Christopher Robin's bedtime prayer is all too typical:

> God bless Mummy – I know that's right.
> Wasn't it fun in the bath tonight?
> The cold so cold, and the hot so hot –
> Oh, God bless Daddy, I quite forgot.

Spell or prayer, witch or Christian, single-minded concentration is essential if it is to work.

One time-honoured way of fixing the intent in your mind is to express it in verse. It does not have to be great poetry – jog-trot doggerel will do. John the Sailor uses this method a lot, repeating the doggerel ' ... until it spins in my mind of its own volition, thereby increasing concentration, preventing my mind from wandering, and blocking out interruptions'.

Let us take a couple of examples. Suppose you are under psychic attack; we discussed the principles of psychic self-defence in the last chapter, but it can help if you have a method of reaffirming your defence 'at the touch of a button' at odd moments in your active life, without having to break off and recapitulate in your mind all the measures you have taken. How about this instantly recallable jingle?

> Shield of the Goddess
> On my arm –
> Psychic arrows
> Cannot harm!

Or you've worked a spell for a job you've applied for, and are on the way to the interview with a touch of stage-fright:

> Clear head, cool mind,
> Nervousness is left behind;
> Clear head, keen eyes,
> Nothing takes me by surprise!

Hardly immortal verse, but it does jingle and is easy to repeat over and over till it embeds itself in your subconscious.

Or if you would prefer something from a respected poet, how about this from T.S. Eliot's *The Curse be Ended*?

> 'Round and round the circle
> Completing the charm'
> So the knot be unknotted
> The cross uncrossed
> The crooked made straight
> And the curse be ended.

Christine Best often completes a spell by winding a small cord round her athame while she holds her purpose in mind, and repeating over and over:

I wind, I bind,
This spell be mine!

She then puts her bound athame safely away until the aim is achieved or until she feels the need to recharge it. Since the cord is only small, she finds she can use the athame for other work with the cord still in place as long as it is needed.

Rhythm is a great help in building up power – and not only the rhythm of verse or music. Diana from the Netherlands tells us: 'When I have to send energy to someone or something, I mostly use dancing and certain gestures, often without words.'

If you have musicians in your coven, live musical backing to rituals, including spell-working, can be very helpful in setting and maintaining the atmosphere. But every group should build up a collection of recorded music for Circle work. Cassettes are the handiest, because you can edit as you transfer music to them, repeat short themes to fill the whole length, and so on.

For the concentrated building-up of power required in spell-working, strongly rhythmic music can be effective – particularly if the music itself builds up as it develops (as with Ravel's *Bolero*, for example). And once you know the music, you may be able to time your working so that the power is released at a moment of musical climax; this can be dramatically (and therefore practically) effective.

Except for specific purposes, music with sung or spoken words should in general be avoided; it can introduce thoughts irrelevant to the work in hand – noticeably if the words are clear, but even subconsciously if they are not.

A very useful concept in spell-working is the thought-form – a special type of visualization. This is rather like what psychiatrists call a 'complex', a group of elements in the psyche which have coalesced to form what appears to be an entity with a will of its own, more or less independent of the individual concerned. In psychiatric cases, of course, a complex is typically a malfunction requiring treatment, but in spell-working, such a 'group of elements' can be deliberately created for a positive purpose and kept under control.

An example from our own experience. The major Irish location to which grey seals come every autumn to bear and rear their pups is the Inishkea group of islands off Co. Mayo. In October 1981 some local fishermen, on the excuse that seals were harming the salmon industry, landed there and massacred hundreds of the pups. There was a great public outcry, and the massacre was illegal anyway, since carefully controlled seal-culling, on the rare occasions when it is considered necessary, is the monopoly of government experts.

Volunteers from the Irish Wildlife Federation camped on bleak Inishkea for the pupping seasons of 1982 and 1983 to prevent a repetition. Our coven would have liked to join them, but this was not possible, so we helped in our own way.

In November 1981 we got together and envisaged a thought-form we named Mara (Gaelic for 'of the sea'). Janet painted a picture of her (see Plate 18 in *The Witches' Way*), so that we could all agree on her appearance. In other words, by concentrated group visualization, we created a 'complex' from elements of all our psyches. Having done so, we briefed it – or rather 'her', because we visualized Mara as a distinct personality. We told her: 'You will manifest visually to, and frighten, anyone who tries to harm the seals on or near Inishkea Islands. You will harm no one unless he persists and there is no other way of stopping him.'

Throughout the following year we recharged Mara and repeated her instructions, at each full Moon.

The massacre was not repeated. A sceptic could be forgiven for saying it was the IWF volunteers and public opinion which achieved this and that our efforts were merely well-meaning self-delusion – but for one interesting development. It would seem that Mara obeyed her briefing in the spirit as well as the letter.

After the 1983 pupping season, we were talking to a couple who had been taking supplies to the Inishkea volunteers, in a small boat in very bad weather. They had tried to land at one point but were urgently waved away by a woman standing on the shore. They landed safely farther along, where they were told that (a) if they had tried to land at the first point, they would have ended up on dangerous rock, and (b) there was no way any human could possibly have been there. All the same, the volunteers were not surprised. The same 'woman' had been seen by several people, walking among the seals, who should have shied away from her but didn't. People called her 'the Ghost'.

The couple knew nothing of our spell-working until after they had told us all this, and after they had described the Ghost's physical appearance – which tallied exactly with that of Mara.

As this book was going to press, the worst oil-spillage disaster in American history struck the Gulf of Alaska, threatening the animals and birds of a thousand square miles of ocean. Another job for Mara, we felt; so we held an emergency Circle, recalled and instructed her and sent her on her way to give her help.

An example of the careful choice of appropriate symbolism. We set up the altar in the West, the quarter of Water, and almost exactly the direction of Alaska. The deity-forms chosen were the Irish/Manx sea god Manannán mac Lir (traditionally an ancestor of Janet's mother's family, the Craddocks) and the Greek Thetis. And the music was

*O'cean* by the flautist Larkin, which we can recommend strongly as Circle music for a Water occasion.

Kevin and Ingrid Carlyon of Sussex used a similar thought-form in another animal context. Kevin tells us:

> Our friend Jack, owner of a few acres on Romney Marsh in Kent, asked if we could work a spell to rid his land of foxes; they had been attacking his sheep and causing many problems.
>
> We visited the smallholding and made a large circle of flowers, placed our altar in the North, and performed a half-hour ceremony in which we left a thought-form in the area. It was aimed at foxes and other predatory animals, as were our words in the simple spell that we made for the occasion.
>
> Jack contacted us a few weeks later to let us know that the foxes had not returned and he had had no trouble since.

Thought-forms, like Circles or wax images (see p. 43 below), should never be left to linger once their purpose is fulfilled. They should be thanked for their work and then ritually dissolved, and their elements consciously reabsorbed by the group-members who contributed them.

There is no objection to taking advantage of a thought-form which already exists. Popular fictional characters are often built up into such thought-forms, and if one of them is appropriate to the aim of a spell, making use of it is just as legitimate as invoking an ancient mythological entity or god-form, which after all was built up in the same way. Both are human call-signs to an aspect of reality, charged with power through being visualized and agreed upon by thousands or millions of people.

A modern example will be found in Chapter 15 of Elizabeth St George's book *The Casebook of a Working Occultist*. She tells, in her uniquely exuberant style, how she was unofficially appealed to for help by an American Embassy friend when the Moon-ship *Apollo 13* was in serious trouble. An appropriate thought-form was needed; and who better than Mr Spock of *Star Trek*?

So Elizabeth summoned him, persuaded him to work on *Apollo*'s faulty computer ... and the computer resumed proper functioning, to everyone's bewilderment. According to Elizabeth, one of the astronauts actually saw Mr Spock at work and thought he was hallucinating through lack of oxygen!

The rule about dispersing a thought-form once the aim is achieved obviously does not apply in the case of such 'public property' thought-forms, even if it were possible. (Who could disperse Mr Spock?) The difference is like that between a book you have written yourself and one you have borrowed from a library. But the thought-form must at least be thanked. Elizabeth meticulously thanked Mr Spock and the Powers she had invoked through him. Mr Spock replied: 'I suppose that is logical.'

A very popular form of spell-working, whether solo or group, is cord magic. The cords are a focus for concentration, reinforced by the physical action of using them; and their colour can be chosen for the purpose in mind (see the end of this chapter for colour-meanings).

The most practical cords are the upholstery kind, about a quarter of an inch thick; and the traditional length is nine feet. Every coven should have a collection of these, of different colours. It is a good idea to bind the ends with thread of the same colour, to stop them fraying.

In the commonest form of coven cord magic, the coven sits facing inwards in a circle, with working partners opposite each other. The cords are stretched across the circle, each with a man holding one end and a woman the other. If the numbers are uneven, one woman or one man may hold two cord-ends. If the sexes are not balanced in numbers, a cord may have to have the same sex at each end, in which case one should silently invoke the God and the other the Goddess, by agreement between them or by the High Priestess's decision, before they start.

The cords are looped over each other once at the centre, to give a single focusing-point for everyone to concentrate on.

When all is ready and the cords stretched tight, the coven can work either for a single wish or for individual wishes.

If it is a single wish, the High Priestess names it, tying a knot as she does so. Then each member in turn, deosil, repeats the wish and ties a knot. When all have spoken, the High Priestess condenses the wish into a single key word or very short phrase. This is repeated, round and round the circle, faster and faster to build up the power, until the High Priestess calls 'Drop!' and everyone lets go of the cords at once to discharge it.

If the wishes are individual, they are named one by one, deosil, and everyone ties a knot for each wish, reinforcing it mentally. Again, the wishes can then be concentrated into a single word or short phrase and repeated faster and faster, deosil, until the 'Drop!' command.

A powerful alternative to the speeded-up repetition is for everyone to stand after the first round of statements, and then, still holding the cords, to move faster and faster, deosil, so that the cords rotate like the spokes of a wheel till 'Drop!' is ordered.

After any of these methods, the cords are gathered up and placed on the altar. The knots are not untied until just before the next coven meeting.

A working partnership, or solo workers, can perform their own simplified versions of this cord magic. One cord spell we have come across from several sources is for the couple, or the solo worker, after stating the wish, to tie nine knots in a cord to the following verse:

> By knot of one, the spell's begun.
> By knot of two, it cometh true.
> By knot of three, so mote it be.
> By knot of four, the open door.
> By knot of five, the spell's alive.
> By knot of six, the spell is fixed.
> By knot of seven, the stars of heaven.
> By knot of eight, the stroke of fate.
> By knot of nine, the thing is mine!

An interesting folklore example of knotted-cord magic, again involving the number nine: it used to be a custom to put round the neck of a newborn baby a necklet of nine strands of scarlet silk, knotted at intervals, and to leave it there till teething was safely over.

Some people (and most people some of the time) find no need for material props at all. John the Sailor tells us:

> If there is something I truly desire, and I concentrate on that desire until the intensity of it becomes almost too painful to bear; then release it, it always comes true. It works perfectly well without props and tricks. Candles, cards, black mirrors etc. are beautiful things, but they are not necessary. Similarly, they are not effectual in themselves. A number of occult supply shops have done rather well out of supplying spell kits to gullible people who can be conned into thinking that if they buy a packet of suitable mysterious paraphernalia, it will help them to achieve their heart's desire. Personally, I have found that if the desire is true, the props aren't necessary; and if the desire isn't true, no amount of props will make it so.

He admits that, 'I am not particularly a purist in this respect'; he sometimes works spells just for fun, props and all – 'This is beautiful, but it isn't necessary.'

On the other hand, there are many people to whom visualization is difficult and who find that 'props' – i.e. symbolically appropriate objects – help to make it easier. Such people are by no means necessarily inferior spell-workers. Elen J. Williams asks: 'May I make a plea on behalf of those who can't visualize? They get very disheartened whenever books seems to imply that vivid visualization is both easy and essential to successful magical work. It seems to me that non-visualizers can often formulate the goals quite clearly by other means, and are very effective in raising and directing power.'

Props or no props is a matter of personal choice; the thing to remember is that the props can be helpful as aids to visualization and concentration if you find them so (which is nothing to be ashamed of), but that they have no independent power in themselves. As John points out, if you buy a 'spell kit' in the belief that it will do the job for you, you are being conned.

The phrase 'have no power in themselves' needs qualifying. The 'astral counterpart' (see p. 16) of a physical object can become charged with such power. One's athame, for example, having been consecrated and then used for magical working, maybe for years, is definitely so charged. It is this astral counterpart which one encounters during psychometry – e.g., sensing the history and associations of a piece of personal jewellery, at which some sensitives are very skilled and accurate. So whatever physical objects are used in spell-working, one should consider whether the charge they may carry will help or hinder the aim. In absent healing work, for example, some object intimately connected with the patient can provide an effective link.

It is not always easy to distinguish the psychic effect of such objects from the psychological; but the distinction is usually of academic interest only, since the two overlap and interact.

Crystalline substances have a particular reputation for absorbing and giving out psychic influences; it is as though the mathematically elegant structure of their molecules makes them resonant to precise vibrational frequencies – not only to those of the physical level but also to what are popularly (but more accurately than cynics may realize) known as 'vibes' on the other levels. (The same is true, obviously, of the music used in the Circle.)

Crystals, from common quartz to precious stones, are widely used in psychic healing for this reason, and whole books have been written on the subject. (See Bibliography under Bhattacharyya, Crow, Fernie, Heaps and Sturzaker.) But the crystalline substance which concerns us especially in our present context is salt – the only homogeneous natural substance, apart from the four natural 'elements' of Air, Fire, Water and Earth, which is physically present in every witches' Circle, as it is in every ritual magician's Circle and alchemist's laboratory.

Salt, being incorruptible itself and the only preservative of meat in the centuries before refrigeration, has long been used in magical working as a psychic purifier and protector. Its absorbent and radiant properties are both acknowledged in the ritual blessing of it by witches and magicians (see p. 29). There is good reason to believe that its psychic reputation is justified; but whether or not one accepts this, its psychological associations make it an excellent focus for the purifying and protecting aspects.

If props, tools and symbols are to be used (whether psychologically, psychically or both), it is essential to get the significance of each clear in your mind, as we have just tried to do with salt. Which brings us, first, to the four 'elements' we mentioned above.

We have put the word in quotes to emphasize a point. Witches and magicians are not pre-scientific in their understanding of the world. They know perfectly well that matter can be classified into the hundred-plus elements of the periodic table. When they use the word 'elements' in a magical context (we can drop the quotes from now on, as we are talking in that context), they mean the four aspects which characterize manifestation and activity on all the levels. When one is spell-working, the nature of the objective should determine which tools and symbols we should concentrate on, and the elements are basic to this.

The four elements of Air, Fire, Water and Earth are often summed up in the four Ls – as Life, Light, Love and Law respectively.

Air represents Life, the principle of mind, intelligence, the left-brain, linear-logical faculty, creativity and the healing of functional disorders. It represents fertilization in the inspirational sense. Its polarity tends to emphasize the masculine, God-aspect. Its elemental entities are known as sylphs. Ritual magicians and Cabalists name its guardian as Raphael. The Circle tools which symbolize it are incense and the wand. Its traditional colour is blue. Its quarter is the East, the direction of the dawn of daylight.

Fire represents Light, energy, drive, potency, fertilization in the organic and energizing sense, desire, the healing of organic disorders, the destruction of the outworn or negative. Its polarity tends to emphasize the God-aspect. Its elemental entities are known as salamanders. Its guardian is Michael. Its Circle tools are the sword, athame and candles. Its traditional colour is red. Its quarter is the South, the direction of the noonday Sun.

Water represents Love, relatedness, the right-brain, intuitive function, the cycle of death and rebirth (and therefore of initiation), Nature in its cyclical-growth aspect, the formative womb and the nourishing breast; so its polarity tends to emphasize the Goddess-aspect. Its elemental entities are known as undines. Its guardian is Gabriel. Its Circle tools are the chalice and the cauldron. Its traditional colour is green. Its quarter is the West, the direction of the evening mists and of restorative rest.

Earth represents Law, solidity, reliability, recognition of the inescapable order of things, Nature in its permanence aspect. Its polarity tends to emphasize the Goddess-aspect. Its elemental entities are known as gnomes. Its guardian is Auriel. Its Circle tool is the pentacle. Its traditional colours are yellow or brown. Its quarter is the

North, the direction of Night, when the immensity of the ordered Cosmos is visible.

(It will be noticed that in the balanced equal-armed cross of the Circle, God- and Goddess-aspects face each other; but it should also be remembered that these God- and Goddess-aspects which we have suggested are a matter of emphasis, not of monopoly. There are also plenty of Air and Fire Goddess-functions, and Water and Earth God-functions.)

There are two qualifications to the above. The attribution of sword and athame to Fire, and of wand to Air, is the tradition which we and many others favour – and frankly, we feel it to be in accord with those tools' nature and function. But others follow the Golden Dawn attribution: sword/Air, wand/Fire. What matters is that you should make your own decision and stick to it; and if you are a group, make sure that every member knows it.

The other qualification concerns the southern hemisphere, in particular Australia and New Zealand, to which countries European magical traditions have emigrated and where the Craft is active and growing. There, too, there are differences of practice. Some groups retain the imported European traditions, but others maintain that, since their Sun travels from East to North to West, the quarters of Earth and Fire should be reversed from the European custom; the Wiccan altar should be in the South; the Circle should be cast widdershins (i.e., Sunwise in their latitudes); the seasonal rituals should be moved six months, and so on. We agree with the revisers. Ritual symbolism should relate to your actual environment, not necessarily to the European authorities on your bookshelf.

To return to the use of elemental symbolism in spell-working. One example of its special value is when what really needs to be worked on is not so much a person's problem but the person himself or herself. Almost always the necessary approach can be elementally diagnosed – for example, a quick temper (excess of Fire), inadequate sense of reality (weakness of Earth and/or of Air), smothering possessiveness (distorted Water) and so on. The aim of the spell can thus be defined, and the appropriate symbolism chosen, to restore the balance.

Oils, perfumes and incenses can play a powerful part in setting the appropriate atmosphere for a spell.

A useful book for oil recipes is Tarostar's *The Witch's Formulary and Spellbook*, which gives twenty pages of them – everything from Exodus Oil (to get rid of an unwanted person) to Money Drawing Oil, Road Opener Oil and oils for each of the zodiacal signs and planets. Tarostar's books (see Bibliography) contain malignant as well as justifiable spells and suffer from a clumsy misuse of archaic language ('taketh' and 'blendeth' as imperatives, for example); but they do include some interesting formulae (including half a dozen 'occult floor washes'), a lot of New Orleans folk-magic, and some permissible spells among the questionable ones.

Perhaps the best-known example of a material object being used in spell-working and deliberately charged with psychic (and psychological) power is the wax image.

In fact, of course, it can be made of any material, though 'wax image' has become its popular name, usually with sinister implications of pin-sticking. But it can be, and often is, used for positive purposes such as healing, and in the permissible preventive action of a binding spell (see Chapter XIX). It is also known as a poppet or fith-fath.

On the subject of materials: in magical working, the more natural they are (whether organic or mineral), the better. Beeswax, for example, is preferable to tallow wax. Wool, cotton and silk are far better than synthetic materials such as nylon, because, useful and beautiful as these may be, they are too far removed from their natural origins to hold a psychic charge effectively.

But to return to the image. Its purpose is (a) to provide a psychic link with the person being worked for, and (b) to help in visualization of the aim.

The identification and visualization should start with the making of the image. One effective way of doing this is to make a knitted doll, voicing your aim (or a key word summing it up) with every stitch. Commercially manufactured dolls have the disadvantage that most of them are largely of synthetic material; though children's dolls can become so charged with the owners' feelings about them that, even if they are made entirely of synthetics, a powerful thought-form, rather than an astral counterpart, has been created.

However the image is made, it should if possible incorporate something of the person concerned – anything from hair or nail clippings to a photograph of his or her face on the front of the head. Identification is what matters, not aesthetics.

Image-making for healing should preferably be done while the Moon is waxing or full, and for a binding spell while it is waning or new. You may also make use of the appropriate planetary days and hours; for these, see Appendix 1.

Though solo witches can and do make and use images with success, ideally they should be made by man-and-woman working partners, with or without the aid of the coven. The traditional method is called 'birthing', enacting a dramatized ritual within a Magic Circle, in which the woman gives birth to the image with the man's assistance as both impregnator and 'midwife'. This ritual can be as vivid or symbolic as your actual relationship and sense of what is acceptable dictates. But however it is done, it must be with the maximum concentration, will-power and visualization of the aim.

Before the birthing, the image is taken to the altar, where the couple sprinkle it with consecrated water-and-salt, saying, 'We name thee —, in the names of Cernunnos and Aradia' (or whatever God- and Goddess-forms they are using). After the birthing, the man takes the image again to the altar and makes the Invoking Pentagram of Earth in front of it (see Fig. 2).

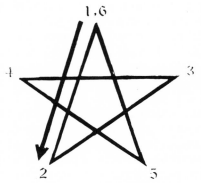

Fig. 2 – Invoking pentagram

Then the couple – and every member of the coven if they are present – in turn take the image and talk to it, reaffirming its identity and repeating the aim of the working.

Finally it is wrapped in cloth and bound with cord, of the appropriate colour (see the end of this chapter), and put in a safe place. It should be taken out of its hiding-place from time to time and the aim reinforced, until that aim is finally achieved.

One last point. When the aim has been achieved or the period of working is over, no image which is identified with a person must be allowed to linger. It must be broken up into pieces, which are taken to naturally flowing water and thrown in, with the instruction 'Return to the elements from which thou camest.'

Jewish tradition, by the way, also included image spells, but only for one purpose – the recovery of stolen property. Jews believed that every person or animal had an 'angelic deputy' assigned to him or her. You pricked an image not to affect someone else directly but to inform your own angelic deputy of the theft and to invoke his help in getting your property back. Your deputy – who would know who the thief was – would then inform the thief's angelic deputy, who would pass the pain of the pricking on to the thief. The thief would then be obliged to return what he had stolen.

Even the Catholic Church used to use wax images – in their case, for exorcism. If someone was believed to be possessed by a demon, the priest would make a wax image of the demon, name and define it and then burn it, reciting suitable verses from Revelation. As the image burned, the demon would leave its victim's body.

'Correspondences' is the word used for objects, creatures, substances, plants, deity-forms, quality-concepts and so on which have a psychic affinity with each other. A study of correspondences is therefore very helpful in planning a spell-working ritual so that everything – accessories, deity-forms invoked, incense, robes if any, colours etc – can be in tune with the operation and contribute to its power.

By far the best, and most widely accepted, compendium of correspondences is Aleister Crowley's book 777. It covers everything from Tarot, animal, plant and Cabalistic lists to the deity-forms of various pantheons.

There simply is not space, here, to go into the subject, because one would not know where to stop. (Though a number of correspondences can be found in the table of Tree of Life sephiroth we give at the end of Chapter VIII.) But two things which tend to enter into even the simplest spell-working are colour – for example, of robes and candles – and number. So perhaps, as a tailpiece to this chapter, these lists of the traditional symbolism of the various colours, and of the basic numbers, will be helpful.

### Colours
WHITE   Purity, innocence, expansion, work for children; Kether on the Tree of Life.

BLACK   Restriction, limitation, binding, secrecy; Saturn; Binah on the Tree of Life. (Black is not sinister in itself; as an absence of colour, it absorbs all colours, and some find that a black robe, for example, makes it easier to absorb into yourself the power and the visualization being built up.)

GOLD, YELLOW   Activity, creativity; Solar magic; the Sun God; Tiphareth on the Tree; in some systems, yellow is the Earth colour. Peter Redgrove, co-author of *The Wise Wound*, tells us that unborn children can sense golden light, which makes this an appropriate colour when working for a pregnant woman.

SILVER   Moon magic; the Moon Goddess; the Goddess in her winter, life-in-death aspect.

RED   Fire; energy, vigour; desire, passion; organic healing; Mars; Geburah on the Tree; the male, electric principle.

ORANGE   Intellect; leadership; communication; travel; Mercury; Hod on the Tree.

GREEN   Nature and its fertility; harmony, equilibrium; the Goddess in her summer, death-in-life aspect; Water; emotion, instinct, intuition; Venus/Aphrodite; Netzach on the Tree.

BLUE   Love, sincerity, loyalty; the Sky Goddess; Air; functional healing; wisdom, justice, organization, administration; Jupiter; Chesed on the Tree; the female, magnetic principle.

VIOLET   Tranquillity; the Akashic Principle; the astral plane; Yesod on the Tree; in some systems, the Spirit colour.

BROWN   Concentration, absorption of knowledge, intuitive communication. Preferred by some to yellow as the Earth colour.

## Numbers

There are really two sets of interpretations of the numbers 1 to 10: first, what we may call the 'traditional' ones listed below, and second, the Cabalistic ones; these correspond to the significances of the ten Sephiroth of the Tree of Life, from Kether (1) to Malkuth (10).

The two approaches differ somewhat – for example, in the traditional interpretations, odd numbers tend to be regarded as male, and even ones as female, which would conflict with the Cabalistic meanings. So if you are spell-working with Cabalistic symbology, refer to Chapter VIII for the appropriate numerological meanings.

1.   Unity. The fundamental source. Strength. Purity. The Ego.

2.   Polarity, and the magic worked by it. Relatedness. Co-operation.

3.   Deity – e.g, the Trinity, the Triple Goddess. The arts. The family (father, mother, child).

4.   Balance. Solidarity. Law. The integration of Heaven and Earth. The four Elements. The cardinal points, orienting and securing the Circle. Organization. Practical achievement.

5.   The four Elements balanced and governed by Spirit. Life. Creativity. Expansion. Exploration.

6.   The focal point of balance. The Hexagram. The principle of 'As above, so below'. Fruitful interaction of the levels. Home-making. Marriage. Co-operation.

7.   Magic. Psychism. Frequently met with in folklore – e.g., the abilities attributed to the seventh child of a seventh child. The still centre in the storm. Time and space, duration, distance.

8.   Leadership in the organizational sense. The anabolic/katabolic process.

9.   Inspiration. Leadership in the communal, compassionate, philanthropic sense. Healing. Humour. Regeneration.

10.   Completeness. Fulfilment. Multiform manifestation. (10 does not feature on its own a great deal in traditional numerology, being regarded as 1+0 and thus a reaffirmation of 1. It is, however, independently important in Cabalism.)

13.   Has to be mentioned alongside 1 to 10 because it appears up so

often in folklore. Generally regarded as unlucky in Christian cultures, maybe partly because Judas was the thirteenth in the team of Jesus and his disciples, and partly from superstitious awe of the number's original magical significance, which seems to have been a Zodiacal one – the twelve aspects in balance, plus the Solar leader. Jesus and his disciples, Robin Hood and his men, Arthur and his Knights, Romulus and his lictors, the Danish hero Hrolf and his berserks are only a few examples of this very frequent pattern. It is interesting that many have a Lunar figure attached to them – Mary, Maid Marian, Morgan/Guinevere and so on; but they are still thought of as thirteen. (Interesting, too, how the Mother-letter M keeps cropping up.) Maybe Christian patriarchy regarded the feminine complement as even more frightening and relegated her (as they did the Virgin Mary) to a subordinate, accessory position.

Thirteen is, of course, the traditional number of that other magical team – the witches' coven. But one wonders whether this was a genuine custom among medieval witches or imposed on them by persecution mythology, simply because the number had come to be regarded as sinister.

# VII  *Sex Magic*

The raising of psychic power is, as we have seen, one of the essentials of spell-working. A precisely understood aim and clear visualization comprise the circuit we set up. With our power-raising, we plug that circuit into the mains so that it can do its job.

One of the power-sources available for this purpose is sex.

Any strong emotion produces an incandescent fireball on the astral plane. In the darker periods of history and in a few diseased corners today, the agony of sacrificial victims (whether animal or human) has been used as a magical power source, with the fireball exploding at the climax of death.

Erotic feeling and activity engender just about the brightest astral fireball (with its explosion at the climax of orgasm) that can legitimately be harnessed to a magical operation.

Legitimately, but with reservations. These can be summed up quite simply. Sex magic without love is black magic. Sex magic should be used only by a couple to whom sex is a normal part of their loving relationship – in other words, by husband and wife or established lovers – and always in private. It should be used within a Magic Circle, even if it has 'only' been cast mentally round the bed.

These rules are not mere conventional morality. They are based on the fact that magic and spell-working involve multi-level reality.

Sexual intercourse between a couple who genuinely love each other activates all the levels simultaneously, from physical to spiritual. Therefore, when such a couple use sex magic, their mating powers the intent of the spell on all these levels, leaving no loose ends or vulnerable areas – which is both more effective and safer. Also, their deep mutual attunement means that their understanding of the intent, and their visualization, will be more completely harmonized.

Casual sex, on the other hand, involves only the physical and astral (usually just the lower astral) levels. These levels are not necessarily 'immoral' – but they tend to be amoral, following their instincts regardless of any consequences other than the immediate gratification of those instincts. And in spell-working, that leaves far too many loopholes.

Sometimes well-intentioned witches, who are friends but do not have a committed sexual relationship, may think that agreed sex magic between them is justified as a means to a legitimate magical end. Unfortunately this will still leave the same loopholes – and it holds dangers for themselves. In the heightened magical atmosphere of spell-working, particularly within a Magic Circle, the intensity of intercourse may trigger off reactions on other levels for which they are not prepared. This might even be more likely, the more well-intentioned they are and the more seriously they take the aim they are working for. At worst, one might be affected more deeply than the other, creating problems for their friendship after the working is over.

Another trap into which some well-intentioned people fall is the attempted use of Tantric magic with totally inadequate knowledge or understanding of that path. Tantra is an Eastern occult system utilizing sexual energy for spiritual development, in which those taking part assume God- and Goddess-forms. It is a complex and subtle system strange to the Western mind, and very effective when properly practised. If you want to get some idea of that complexity, we suggest you read Agehananda Bharati's *The Tantric Tradition* (see Bibliography). But mere book-study is not enough; unless you can learn it from a genuine – preferably Eastern – teacher, it is best left alone.

Regrettably, one must add that there are groups which cannot be called well-intentioned; groups on the fringes of the pagan, occult and witchcraft movement who use that movement to excuse sexual promiscuity for kicks – even involving children. They are a small minority and are in no way genuine pagans, occultists or witches; but they provide welcome ammunition for those bigoted propagandists, both religious and political, who want to present them as typical of the whole and to encourage persecution and even legislation against the movement. The sensationalist media fall for this trick, as mainstream witches and occultists know only too well.

This may seem a digression, but it needs saying, because in the late 1980s the witch-hunt campaign in Britain and America has intensified and become more deliberate and unscrupulous. It has to be countered by stating the mainstream movement's principles clearly and publicly – including the fact that sexual promiscuity, and certainly the abuse of minors, is contrary to those principles. Otherwise we could be driven underground, which is precisely what the sick fringe would like.

Basically, *homo/femina sapiens* is not a promiscuous species but a pair-bond one – like other mammals such as gorillas, badgers and wolves, and almost all birds. (The colloquialism 'wolf' for a determinedly promiscuous man is a gross slander on that species, as any zoologist will confirm! A male pack-leader may have more than one mate, but the relationship with each is continuing, not promiscuous.) Even in polygamous human or animal societies (and the rare polyandrous human ones, such as in parts of the Himalayas where the men are seasonally mobile and the women static), the same emphasis on permanence and continuity is evident.

Since occultism and witchcraft believe in discovering our true nature and developing it, this basic characteristic of our species is worth bearing in mind.

Enough of the moral dimension, which should be clear by now; back to sex magic itself.

There are two forms of male–female magical working, which we have come to call 'gender magic' and 'sex magic'.

Gender magic, which is a basic element of most witchcraft covens, utilizes the essential creative polarity of man and woman, each contributing his or her basic gender-emphasis as a channel for the God- and Goddess-principles, man and woman being the complementary terminals of the magical battery which allow the current, the magical power, to flow effectively. In a way, it is like ballroom dancing, in that it does not have to be 'sexual' in the narrow sense; brother and sister, mother and son, or father and daughter can work as magical partners just as innocently and effectively as they can partner each other on the dance floor.

Sex magic, on the other hand, involves intercourse, or mutual erotic desire short of intercourse, as the source of magical power.

These two approaches are typified in the two versions of that hallowed Wiccan ritual, the Great Rite (see our *Eight Sabbats for Witches*, pp. 48–54, or *The Witches' Way*, pp. 31–9). The 'symbolic' Great Rite, using the athame and chalice, is gender magic; the 'actual' Great Rite, involving intercourse, is sex magic.

(The Great Rite given in *The Witches' Way* is the full text from Gerald Gardner's own *Book of Shadows* in the possession of Doreen Valiente; the version in *Eight Sabbats for Witches* is a simpler form as we were taught it by our own initiators, Alex and Maxine Sanders, but possibly also Gardnerian in origin. For ourselves, we find the full-text version too complicated and verbose for natural working; few people could learn it all by heart, and book-in-hand detracts from the dignity and drama. We always use the simpler version, whether symbolic or actual, and are very happy with it. But this is a matter for individual choice.)

The purpose of sex magic, whether by the 'actual' Great Rite in a formal Circle or less ritually in bed (or wherever) in a mentally cast circle, is simple: the harnessing of the great multi-level power of harmonious intercourse for a given magical aim.

As always, that aim should be precisely defined and visualized beforehand; and with sex magic this is particularly important, because once the mutual arousal has started, the couple should not be distracted by nagging uncertainties. The definition of the precise aim should have settled any such uncertainty already and should be recallable instantly and vividly at the moment of release of power, by a simple trigger phrase and/or vivid image.

Little need be said about that mutual arousal, because if the couple are (as they should be) attuned to each other and fully aware of each other's needs, likes and dislikes, these will be unique to them, and lecturing them on the subject would be presumptuous. But the arousal should be uninhibited and directed towards the maximum building-up of expectant tension – not merely as is often quite legitimately the case in love-making, towards the release of tension that is already there.

Orgasm is the moment at which to call up the visualization of the magical aim and to release the build-up of power for that purpose.

Simultaneous orgasm is, of course, ideal for this, but it is not always achievable (many couples are quite happy with one-after-the-other, and why not?), and trying to achieve it should never reach the level of worrying about it, which would inhibit the power-building. If the orgasms are separate, both partners should visualize the release of the power of each orgasm as it happens; not an easy technique for some to learn, but worth perfecting. If your partner comes first, a helpful key is to tell yourself that the release of his or her power is exciting and stimulating for you too, and therefore builds up your own power still further. If he or she comes second, realize that your own post-orgasmic pleasure is a firm foundation, a kind of launching-pad, for the effective release of the power of his or her excitement.

Many women do not have an orgasm every time they make love, but still find the non-orgasmic occasions satisfying (a fact which men, whose physiology requires ejaculation, often fail to understand). If this happens during sex-magic intercourse, on no account should the woman feel guilty or inadequate. She should, again, visualize her own particular form of pleasure as a launching-pad, and her man's orgasm as a perfectly adequate moment for the release of the power which their sexual polarity has built up. She can even tell herself that 'someone up there' has decided that this particular syndrome is best for the purpose in hand – and she may well be right. Faith in the gods' and goddesses' purpose makes it easier for them to use us as channels.

As we explained on p. 172 of *The Witches' Way*, post-coital reverie also has a magical use. There we were talking about the couple's own benefit, but it can also be used to help others. There are occasions (more about this on p. 71 of the present book) when the most effective spell-working for a friend is the projection of love, reassurance and calm; and what better frame of mind for that than the glowing peace which follows harmonious love-making?

Are there occasions on which several couples may take part in a sex-magic working?

Yes, there are, when maximum power is needed, but the same rules apply: that each couple must be married or established lovers – and, in addition, each couple should have their own island of privacy, which in practice usually means a very large Circle, out of doors, in the dark.

Maxine Sanders gives two examples from her own experience, in Chapter 9 of her book *Maxine: The Witch Queen*. The first was a Spring Equinox ritual on the Yorkshire moors many years ago, when power was raised to send help to various people. The second was by five couples in a London flat, to save a child who was dying of cancer.

'When the lights were finally lit again there was a feeling of great happiness and achievement,' Maxine records.

'The child? It recovered. Doctors don't like this kind of "miracle". I don't think they ever really convinced themselves that it was the same child. She's beautiful now, quite beautiful.'

Maxine calls such workings 'sacred orgies' and admits that the phrase is often 'bandied about by people who lack understanding, or the will to understand what is meant'.

A pertinent warning, with which we agree. The small, sick fringe who use the Craft as an excuse for a gang-bang, without either love or

privacy, should remember that (a) any intended magic won't work and
(b) they are not only running the risk of physical disease but inviting
mental and spiritual disease as well.

In the ancient pagan world, one widespread form of sex magic was the
*hieros gamos* or sacred marriage.

In its most characteristic form, it involved ritual intercourse
between a king or leader and a priestess of the appropriate goddess –
of sovereignty to confirm his kingship, of fertility to ensure that of his
people's territory, or of victory to ensure its defence. The story of
Esther and King Ahasuerus in the Book of Esther (the only book in
the Bible, apart from the Song of Solomon, which never mentions the
Jewish God) is, in fact, an unmistakable record of such a pagan *hieros
gamos*. So is the Irish legend of Queen Medhbh (Maeve) of Connacht,
who must originally have been a priestess of the goddess of
sovereignty, or a memory of all such priestesses; she was said to have
been the wife of nine kings of Ireland, and only a man who had mated
with her could be king. To judge by her legends, she must also have
personified the warrior goddess; and it is perhaps ironic that she has
finished up in English folklore as the Queen Mab of fairy-tale.

A happy tradition still to be found in many places is the choosing of
a girl as Queen of the May for the village, or wherever, with
appropriate enthroning and parading and general celebration. But this
innocent festival, too, is a direct descendant of a *hieros gamos*. In the
old days, a King of the May would also be chosen, and the couple's
union would be publicly and ritually consummated in a newly sown
field.

As Sir James Frazer put it in *The Golden Bough* (pp. 178–9 of the
abridged edition – see Bibliography), such rituals ' ... were charms
intended to make the woods to grow green, the fresh grass to sprout,
the corn to shoot, and the flowers to blow.... Accordingly we may
assume with a high degree of probability that the profligacy which
notoriously attended these ceremonies was at one time not an
accidental excess but an essential part of the rites, and that in the
opinion of those who performed them the marriage of trees and plants
could not be fertile without the real union of the human sexes.'

Another example of the *hieros gamos* will be found on p. 147.

Finally, we would point out what should be obvious: that the
Wiccan Great Rite, particularly when used as a man's third-degree
initiation ritual, is itself a *hieros gamos*. The woman, who has been the
subject of Drawing Down the Moon, personifies the goddess of
initiation; and if he approaches the occasion in the right spirit, by his
mating with her (whether symbolic or actual) the man confirms and
validates his new status.

Which provokes a thought: when it is the woman who is receiving her third degree, might it not be appropriate to Draw Down the Sun (see *The Witches' Way*, Chapter VI) on the man, to emphasize that for her, and for the same purpose, he represents the god of initiation?

# VIII  *Spell-Working and the Cabala*

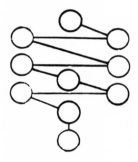

The Cabala (also spelled with a Q or a K) is a philosophical and magical system intrinsic to the Western mystery tradition. It is Hebrew in origin, and its technical terms are still Hebrew. In Western use, its teachings have undergone some changes of emphasis but, as Dion Fortune put it (*The Mystical Qabalah*, p. 2), they are the 'legitimate descendants' and 'natural development' of the originals.

The Cabala is not generally regarded as a part of mainstream Wiccan tradition; some witches find it helpful, while others make a point of avoiding it. But in the present opening-up of occult information and discussion it has certainly interacted with the Craft; and there is some evidence of such interaction from earlier times, through contact between witches and magicians (and also, through sympathetic contact as persecuted minorities, between witches and Jews).

We are among those who find Cabalistic concepts a fruitful expansion of 'pure' witchcraft (if there is such a thing). From the point of view of spell-working, which is our concern here, it can provide a very useful framework for sorting out and clarifying preparatory thinking, and also a rich source of correspondences and related symbols for the actual working.

Whether you find the same is up to you. There are countless good, intelligent and effective witches who make no use of it at all. The best thing we can suggest is that you read this chapter carefully, ask yourself if it rings a bell with you, and either take it from there or put it aside. It is to offer you this choice that we have included this chapter.

It is impossible, here, to do more than outline the principles of the Cabala very briefly. For a proper grounding, the best single book is Dion Fortune's *The Mystical Qabalah*, quoted above.

The basic blueprint of Cabalistic thinking is its Tree of Life, shown in Figure 3. It represents the fundamental aspects and categories of being – whether in terms of cosmic creation and evolution or in the make-up of an individual, a situation or a process of development.

It is a glyph or diagram consisting of ten spheres or Sephiroth (singular, Sephira), with Kether ('The Crown') at the top and Malkuth ('The Kingdom') at the bottom. These are connected with each other in two ways: (1) by the sequence from Kether to Malkuth, reading downwards and from right to left; and the same sequence in the reverse direction. This is known as 'The Lightning Path'; (2) by a network of twenty-two Paths linking certain sephiroth.

There are also two ways of grouping the Sephiroth:

(1) Into three triangles – the Supernal Triangle at the top, consisting of Kether, Chokmah and Binah; this is separated by the Abyss from the Ethical Triangle in the middle, consisting of Chesed, Geburah and Tiphareth; the Astral Triangle below this, consisting of Netzach, Hod and Yesod. This leaves Malkuth, representing the Material World.

(2) Into three pillars – the Pillar of Mercy on the right, consisting of Chokmah, Chesed and Netzach; the Pillar of Severity on the left, consisting of Binah, Geburah and Hod; and the Middle Pillar, of Mildness or Equilibrium, consisting of Kether, Tiphareth, Yesod and Malkuth.

The essential theme of the Tree, on a macrocosmic scale, is the Involution from the pure existence of Kether, following the Lightning Path down to physical manifestation in Malkuth; and the Evolution back to the source, enriched by the experience of manifestation, along the Lightning Path upwards.

On a microcosmic scale, it represents the balance of aspects within an individual or a situation, and their interaction. But on either scale, the old Cabalistic saying must always be remembered: 'All the Sephiroth are equally holy.'

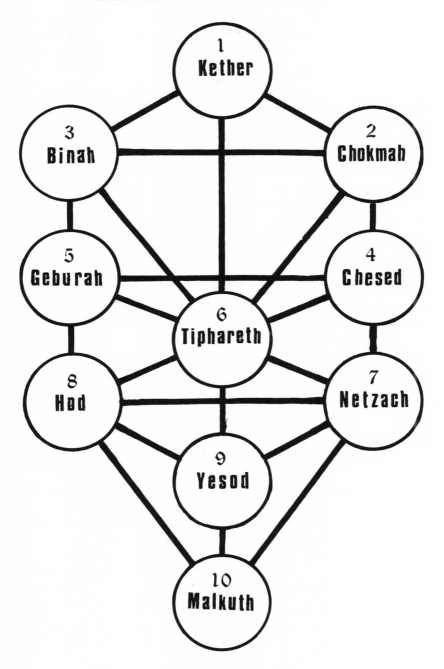

Fig. 3 – The Tree of Life

The lower end of the Tree of Life is not 'evil' or morally inferior. Physical manifestation is an essential aspect of the cosmic process, one of its ways of accumulating experience and complexity; and at the human level, the body merits as much respect and enjoyment as the spirit.

Each Sephira has a host of correspondences; the most comprehensive listing of these is in Aleister Crowley's 777.

The Tree can also be considered in four Worlds or levels: Atziluth, the Archetypal World; Briah, the Creative World; Yetzirah, the Formative World; and Assiah, the Material World.

These Worlds can be thought of in two ways. First, one may envisage each World as embracing its own complete Tree, the Malkuth of Atziluth giving rise to the Kether of Briah, and so on. And second, the Tree itself can be divided between the Worlds: Atziluth being Kether; Briah being Chokmah and Binah; Yetzirah being Chesed, Geburah, Tiphareth, Netzach, Hod and Yesod; and Assiah being Malkuth. Both these approaches are valid (and sometimes both at once), according to context.

The twenty-two Paths connecting the Sephiroth are a study on their own, too complex to go into here. Briefly, each Path represents the creative interaction and balance between the two Sephiroth it connects. Their correspondences include the twenty-two Major Arcana of the Tarot.

Going deeper, one can think of each Sephira as containing a complete Tree of its own. Thus one can consider the Geburah aspect of Chesed, the Netzach aspect of Yesod, and so on. (This is not quite the same as considering the Paths between those Sephiroth.)

Associated with each Sephira is a Qlipha (plural Qliphoth), its negative and destructive aspect, arising when it is not balanced by the other Sephiroth – creative balance being the whole meaning of the Tree.

Here are brief summaries of the natures of the ten Sephiroth, with some of their symbols and correspondences. (Note: there are four different colour scales for the Sephiroth, corresponding to the four Worlds: the King Scale, in Atziluth; the Queen Scale, in Briah; the Emperor Scale, in Yetzirah; and the Empress Scale, in Assiah. The colours given below are those of the Queen Scale, which are the most widely used in practical magic.)

1. KETHER ('The Crown'): The First Manifest; pure existence, without form. Microcosmically, the ultimate essence of an individual or a situation – though 'individuality' and 'situation' can only really be conceived in relation to the Tree as a whole.
Magical Image: An ancient bearded king seen in profile.

Cosmic/Astrological: Primum Mobile, the First Swirlings.
Spiritual Experience: Union with the Divine.
Virtue: Attainment. Completion of the Great Work.
Vice: None.
Symbols: The Point. The Crown. The Swastika (not the reversed swastika of the Nazis but rotating the other way).
Tarot Cards: The four Aces, roots of the powers of each element.
Colour: Pure white brilliance.

2.   CHOKMAH ('Wisdom'): The Supernal Father. Pure, directionless energy, still without form; the Great Stimulator and Impregnator.
Magical Image: A bearded male figure.
Cosmic/Astrological: The Zodiac.
Spiritual Experience: The Vision of Divinity face to face.
Virtue: Devotion.
Vice: None.
Symbols: The Phallus. The Yod of the Tetragrammaton. The Standing-stone. The Straight Line.
Tarot Cards: The four Twos (Wands, Dominion; Cups, Love; Swords, Peace Restored; Pentacles, Harmonious Change).
Colour: Grey.

3.   BINAH ('Understanding'): The Supernal Mother. Takes the directionless energy of Chokmah and gives it form by confining it within limits. Binah is thus the ultimate root of matter: 'Malkuth sitteth upon the throne of Binah.' The Dark Mother in the sense of necessary constriction and confinement to create form, and death to produce rebirth. Chokmah and Binah together are the basic creative polarity of the cosmos.
Magical Image: A mature woman.
Spiritual Experience: Vision of Sorrow.
Cosmic/Astrological: Saturn.
Virtue: Silence.
Vice: Avarice.
Symbols: The Yoni. The Cup or Chalice.
Tarot Cards: The four Threes (Wands, Established Strength; Cups, Abundance; Swords, Sorrow; Pentacles, Material Works).
Colour: Black.

(Between this Supernal Triangle and the rest of the Tree comes the ABYSS – a demarcation in the nature of being, between the potential and the actual. Actual manifestation, as our finite minds can conceive it, begins below the Abyss. In the Abyss is the 'Invisible Sephira', DAATH, which may be thought of as the Sephira of Becoming.)

4.   CHESED ('Mercy'). Also known as GEDULAH. The loving Father, protector and preserver; Chokmah on a lower arc; organization, the benevolent ruler. Formulation of archetypal ideas; the source of inspiration to be worked out on the planes of form.
Magical Image: A mighty crowned and throned king.
Cosmic/Astrological: Jupiter.
Spiritual Experience: Vision of Love.
Virtue: Obedience.
Vice: Bigotry, hypocrisy, gluttony, tyranny.
Symbols: The Solid Figure. The Tetrahedron. The Pyramid. The Equal-armed Cross. Orb. Wand. Sceptre. Crook.
Tarot Cards: The four Fours (Wands, Perfected Work; Cups, Pleasure; Swords, Rest from Strife; Pentacles, Earthly Power).
Colour: Blue.

5.   GEBURAH ('Strength, Severity'): The Katabolic, or downbreaking, aspect of force, which eliminates the outworn aspects. The Army to Chesed's Government. The dragon-slayer. Geburah, though awe-inspiring, is not 'evil'; it is the necessary breaking-down, the Katabolic aspect of the life-process, concerned with the release of force in activity.
Magical Image: A mighty warrior in his chariot.
Cosmic/Astrological: Mars.
Spiritual Experience: Vision of Power.
Virtue: Energy, courage.
Vice: Cruelty, destruction.
Symbols: The Pentagon. The five-petalled Tudor rose. The Sword. The Spear. The Scourge. The Chain.
Tarot Cards: The four Fives (Wands, Strife; Cups, Loss in Pleasure; Swords, Defeat; Pentacles, Earthly Trouble).
Colour: Scarlet.

6.   TIPHARETH ('Beauty'): The centre of equilibrium of the whole Tree; the point of transmutation between the planes of force and the planes of form; Kether on a lower arc and Yesod on a higher arc. The ruler of the six Sephiroth of Yetzirah, the Formative World. The Place of Incarnation; in terms of the reincarnating human, the four Sephiroth above Tiphareth represent the Individuality, or immortal self, and Kether its Divine Spark, while the four Sephiroth below Tiphareth represent the Personality, or lower self of each incarnation. Tiphareth integrates the two. The Sacrificed God; in Christian terms, the Christ Sephira: 'Tiphareth the Son showeth us Kether the Father.'
Magical Image: A majestic king. A child. A sacrificed god.
Cosmic/Astrological: The Sun.
Spiritual Experience: Vision of the Harmony of Things.

Virtue: Devotion to the Great Work.
Vice: Pride.
Symbols: The Lamen. The Rosy Cross. The Calvary Cross. The truncated Pyramid. The Cube.
Tarot Cards: The four Sixes (Wands, Victory; Cups, Joy; Swords, Earned Success; Pentacles, Material Success).
Colour: Yellow.

7. NETZACH ('Victory'). Instincts and emotions; force on a lower scale, balanced by Hod, which is form on a lower scale. Or rather 'not force, but forces; not life, but lives' (Dion Fortune). The Sephira of Nature, the arts, dance, sound and colour. The right-brain, intuitive function. In Netzach and Hod, thought-forms take shape and manifest in Yesod. Netzach and Hod are an essential balanced polarity, just like Chesed and Geburah.
Magical Image: A beautiful naked woman.
Cosmic/Astrological: Venus.
Spiritual Experience: Vision of Beauty Triumphant.
Virtue: Unselfishness.
Vice: Promiscuity, lust.
Symbols: Lamp and Girdle. The Rose.
Tarot Cards: The four Sevens (Wands, Valour; Cups, Illusory Success; Swords, Unstable Effort; Pentacles, Success Unfulfilled.
Colour: Emerald.

8. HOD ('Glory'): Intellect, the form-giving imagination; the left-brain, linear-logical function. The Sephira of magical working – of formulating forms in the mind and of using the will to link with the natural forces of Netzach to ensoul those forms. Formal magic as opposed to simple mind power.
Magical Image: A hermaphrodite.
Cosmic/Astrological: Mercury.
Spiritual Experience: Vision of Splendour.
Virtue: Truthfulness.
Vice: Falsehood, dishonesty.
Symbols: Names and Versicles and Apron.
Tarot Cards: The four Eights (Wands, Swiftness; Cups, Abandoned Success; Swords, Shortened Force; Pentacles, Prudence).
Colour: Orange.

9. YESOD ('Foundation'). The receptacle of the emanations of all the Sephiroth above it, which it 'purifies and corrects'. The Akashic principle, the Astral Ether. The Sephira of the Machinery of the Universe, the last stage before physical manifestation. The

treasure-house of images, and also the sphere of Maya, or illusion. Reflects the light of Tiphareth as the Moon does that of the Sun. Rhythmic, like the Moon and the menstrual cycle.
Magical Image: A beautiful naked man, very strong.
Cosmic/Astrological: The Moon.
Spiritual Experience: Vision of the Machinery of the Universe.
Virtue: Independence.
Vice: Idleness.
Symbols: The Perfumes and Sandals.
Tarot Cards: The four Nines (Wands, Great Strength; Cups, Material Happiness; Swords, Despair and Cruelty; Pentacles, Material Gain).
Colour: Violet.

10.    MALKUTH ('Kingdom'): The Sephira of Earth, of physical manifestation – but also of the Earth-Soul, of the subtle, psychic aspect of matter. Yesod depends for the manifestation of its activities on the substance provided by Malkuth; equally, Malkuth is inanimate matter till Yesod ensouls it. Here Involution reaches completion, and Evolution begins. 'Every magical operation must come through to Malkuth before it can be reckoned to have attained completion, for only in Malkuth is force finally locked home into form' (Dion Fortune).
Magical Image: A young woman, crowned and throned.
Cosmic/Astrological: Sphere of the Elements.
Spiritual Experience: Vision of the Holy Guardian Angel.
Virtue: Discrimination.
Vice: Avarice. Inertia.
Symbols: Altar of the double Cube. The Equal-armed Cross. The Magic Circle. The Triangle of Art.
Tarot Cards: The four Tens (Wands, Oppression; Cups, Perfected Success; Swords, Ruin; Pentacles, Wealth).
Colour: Citrine, olive, russet and black (the four elements).

# IX  *Talismans*

A talisman is, so to speak, the concentration of the meaning and intent of a spell into a pocketable or wearable form. It is a personal thing, for the protection, encouragement, strengthening or what-have-you of the individual who carries or wears it.

It is much more tailor-made than a mere amulet, which is generalized, such as the traditional rabbit's foot or St Christopher medal. (The *Shorter Oxford English Dictionary* defines an amulet simply as 'Anything worn as a charm against evil, disease, witchcraft, etc.'; its definition of a talisman is much longer, involving the engraving of planetary symbols and so on, and its use to bring good fortune as well as to avert evil, and says it is 'usually worn as an amulet'.)

The same rules apply to a talisman as to spell-working in general. It must be for a specific purpose, precisely visualized and defined. Imagination must be called upon for its creation. And maximum will-power must go into its charging.

Fig. 4 – A typical Talisman

The method we have found most satisfactory for creating a talisman is what may be called the four-page system.

Out of a sheet of strong paper – or, even better, parchment – folded once, cut two circles about three inches in diameter and hinged together at one side, so that it can be folded like a book into a single pocketable disc. This provides four surfaces for the drawing of appropriate symbols.

Figure 4 shows a typical example. Let us say a townee called Joan Hume is moving to the country, of which she has no experience. She is anxious to attune herself to it as quickly as possible and to learn to interact with Nature in a way that benefits both herself and her new environment. So a witch friend (we'll call her Sally) has made her this talisman to help her succeed in her resolve.

Side 1 is Joan's name plotted on the planetary square of the Sun, chosen because it is the one most directly related to the fruitfulness of the Earth and the cycle of the seasons. To understand this name-plotting, look at Appendix 2 on pp. 166–70. First, the numerological equivalent of Joan's name is found from the table on p. 167. It turns out to be

$$\begin{array}{cccc cccc} J & O & A & N & H & U & M & E \\ 1 & 6 & 1 & 5 & 8 & 3 & 4 & 5 \end{array}$$

This sequence is then traced in a continuous line from number to number over the Sun square on p. 167 (or over a scaled-down copy of it appropriate to the size of the talisman), which produces the figure you see. (For the scaled-down copy, the simplest way is to draw it lightly in pencil directly onto the talisman – without the numbers, which you can read from the original – and to erase this once the name-sigil has been plotted in ink.) In this way, any name can be plotted on any of the seven planetary squares, to symbolize the harmonizing of the person with the qualities the planet represents.

Joan and Sally both knew it was obvious that Joan must attune herself to the animal and plant aspects of her new surroundings; so these took up sides 2 and 3.

To symbolize the animal aspect, Sally chose a squirrel; she knew there were some in Joan's area, and it would do her good to keep her eyes open for the shy creatures. For the plant aspect, she drew an acorn – not merely because there were oaks around but because the acorn's phallic shape has always been a symbol of fertility. (She did not mention the latter reason to Joan, leaving it to work on her subconscious!)

One thing Sally realized more clearly than Joan was that her attunement to Nature must include what is perhaps its most basic characteristic – the fact that it is cyclic and rhythmic. So for side 4 she chose a simple circle of four curved arrows to represent the eternal cycle of the seasons, embracing the ankh, symbol of life.

We cannot show the colours in our figure, but of course Sally used these to emphasize the symbolism. For side 1, with its solar connotation, she would have liked to use gold ink, but she knew that this rubs off easily, and she wanted the finished talisman to retain its brightness, so she settled for orange.

For side 2, she drew the squirrel in red, the colour of animal life-blood – another reason for choosing the squirrel, because it was red anyway. For the acorn, she used the green of plant fertility.

For side 3, she drew the four arrows in green, orange, brown and black, in deosil order, to symbolize spring, summer, autumn and winter; and the ankh she drew in bright blue.

Finally, she made a little sachet of silk to hold the talisman, and told Joan to wear it all day (' ... tucked in your bra next to your heart if you don't sweat too much – don't want the ink to run') and keep it under her pillow at night. Once a day she must take it out and study each side in turn, to absorb its meaning.

This four-sided paper or parchment disc is not the only form a talisman can take, of course. It can be a ring, a piece of engraved metal, wood or stone – anything, so long as it is tailor-made for its purpose.

A very simple good-fortune talisman is a little red bag into which you put a pinch of salt, a piece of cloth, a tiny lump of coal, a piece of silk cut into the shape of a heart, a silver sixpence if you can get one (if not, any small coin) and a small piece of bread. When everything is inside, you sew the bag up with red woollen thread, reciting as you sew:

> This bag I sew for luck for me,
> And also for my family,
> That it may keep by night and day
> Trouble and illness far away.
> Flags, flax, fodder and frig!

The last line is an old Craft wish. The four words mean, respectively, a roof over your head; clothes for your back; food for your belly; and a happy sex-life (from the Nordic love goddess Frigg). This verse is, of course, a formula for blessing the talisman; and every talisman – or, come to that, amulet – should be ritually blessed or consecrated before it is put to use.

This requirement is as old as magic itself; here, for example, is an ancient Chaldaean blessing of a talisman to protect a house:

'Talisman, talisman, boundary that cannot be taken away, boundary that the gods cannot pass, barrier irremovable, which is opposed to malevolence! – whether it be a wicked Utuq, a wicked Alal, a wicked Gigim, a wicked god, a Maskim, a phantom, a spectre, a vampire, an incubus, a succubus, a nightmare, may the barrier of the god Ea stop him!' (Utuk, Alal and so on are various categories of evil spirits, while Ea was the Chaldaean and Assyro-Babylonian god of water, wisdom and magic.)

The usual method of consecration in the Craft today is with the four elements, within a Magic Circle. One person, or preferably a man and woman, places the object on the pentacle on the altar, with their hands over it, saying: 'I [we] consecrate thee with the element of Earth'; then sprinkle it with consecrated water, using the corresponding phrase; then pass it through the incense smoke for Air, again with the appropriate words; and finally (at a safe distance) over the candle flame for Fire. The declaration here ends with 'in the names of Cernunnos and Aradia' or whatever suitable deity names have been chosen. If it is being done by a man and a woman, finally they embrace and kiss with the object held between their chests by the pressure of their bodies – being careful not to drop it as they separate.

Talismans can be an effective method of personal protection. Eric Winch from Norwich tells us:

> A female acquaintance asked for protection from a man who appeared to be taking an unhealthy interest in her when she travelled by train to work. It's not that he had touched her; in fact he hadn't even spoken to her. His looks were hostile and threatening.
>
> I cast a spell and made her a talisman to wear around her waist, tied with suitably coloured ribbons. The talisman consisted of runic symbols of protection, and her own zodiac glyphs. From the very first day that she wore it, the man seemed to lose interest in her, and a few days later sat in a different compartment from her.

As with other spells, with talismans it is often the person concerned who must be worked on, rather than his or her external dangers or problems. They can be useful, for example, in countering hang-ups or phobias which are creating difficulties. Elen J. Williams tells us: 'A particularly successful piece of work involved making a talisman for a person who was agoraphobic; it was effective for years until the talisman wore out. A quick repair job restored its efficiency!'

One talisman or amulet which has remained in the possession of the same family for six centuries or more is the Lee Penny or Lee Stone. It is a groat of the reign of Edward I (1272–1307), with a small dark red triangular stone on the reverse side. It belongs to the Scottish family

Lee of Lockhart and is said to have been brought back from the Holy Land by their ancestor Sir Simon Lockart early in the fourteenth century.

Water into which the Lee Penny was dipped and turned was said to cure rabies, haemorrhaging, cattle ailments and other diseases. Newcastle-on-Tyne borrowed it in 1645 during an outbreak of plague, with the then huge bond of £6,000 for its safe return. The city must have been satisfied with the results, because they offered to buy it afterwards, but the family would not sell.

Seven years before this, Glasgow Synod had investigated a charge of witchcraft against the Lee family because of the Penny. They decided that it did seem to have healing powers, ' ... whereof no human witt can give a reason, it having pleasit God to give to stones and herbes special virtues for the healing of mony infirmities in man and beast'. They absolved the Lees, since no spoken charms were used, but prudently advised the Laird of Lee ' ... to take heed that it be used hereafter with the least scandal that possiblie may be'.

Another Scottish talisman of this kind was the Lockerbie Penny, a flat piece of silver belonging to a family who lived at Lockerbie in Dumfriesshire. It too had to be dipped in water, which then acquired its healing power – specifically for hydrophobia in cattle. It was often lent to neighbouring farmers when a cow or donkey had been bitten by a mad dog. In 1844 the *Gateshead Observer* reported that, owing to the appearance of seven mad dogs in the area, a large supply of Lockerbie water was sent for 'by public subscription'. (It was referred to here as 'Lockerlee Water', but it was clearly the same.)

Talismans and amulets are used not only for humans; the outstanding examples of their use for animals are horse-brasses. Nowadays people tend to regard them as purely decorative, and they certainly are that, but their original purpose was to protect the horse against malign spell-working. Their designs, which have remained traditional even today, are all of good-luck, life-enhancing symbolism, such as rayed Suns, crescent Moons, horseshoes (points downwards in this context – see p. 117) and so on – mostly pagan, or at least not specifically Christian.

Horse-brasses belonged to the carter, not to the boss, and were handed down from father to son. The full set could be as many as twenty pieces, worn only on gala days; one or two (very probably chosen for the nature of the work in hand or to counter a suspected threat) would be enough protection for an ordinary day.

# X  *Coming Unstuck*

It should be clear by now that the principal reason for a spell's producing unwanted results is unprecise formulation, and for actual failure, insufficient thought about what is really needed.

Susa Morgan Black gives an embarrassing example of the latter: 'I know of a man who wanted very badly to be notorious and get his name in the newspaper. Unfortunately, one night he got drunk and rowdy, was arrested and found his name in the paper under "Arrests". So the key word when working spells is – be specific – or at least include the clause "May only good come of this spell for all involved." '

Eric Winch from Norwich gives us an example of the results of insufficient thought and hasty working. A young friend of his

> ... was short-listed for a job with a local radio station, and asked for a spell that would ensure him the job. This as we know would have been the wrong approach; the only way would be to work on the selection

board to see whether he was the right man for the job. In a hurry, without much due thought, I cast a spell one lunchtime.

The board found none of the candidates suitable and re-advertised the job. The young man re-applied, and again was short-listed, and this time I spent more time and thought on the working. It meant that I had to rise early enough from my bed to cast the spell at three o'clock in the morning. I am happy to say that he got the job.

One should always make sure one is aware of all the circumstances before working a spell; leaping to conclusions may miss the real nature of the problem. Eric gives us an example of this, too:

A friend of mine was going through a very deep low. The slightest upset or harsh word reduced her to tears. Hoping to boost her from this low to a high, I worked a spell to suit. Finding that red was a colour deficient in her planetary natal signs, I included much of that colour with Mars and Aries in a talisman.

However, instead of increasing her confidence, it only made her worse. Then I discovered the root of the problem. Her working environment caused the depression. Working from this angle, that is at bringing about change in that area, some alterations in the timetable were made, and as a result she returned to her usual cheerful self. Her departmental head suddenly realized that the timetable was out of date, and a change was long overdue.

Spells which are successful in themselves may sometimes have unexpected side-effects or 'overspill'. Elen J. Williams tells us of such a case ' ... when we worked to help a coven member become pregnant. We got a clear impression that she would be pregnant within six months, which she was. However, another member who had no intention of having a child also became pregnant. After the initial shock she decided she rather liked the idea!'

Visualization, as we have seen, is a powerful element in spell-working; but it must be appropriate or its power may work in unexpected and sometimes unwanted ways. Merlin and Morgana in the Netherlands give us an example:

It concerns a young woman who was unemployed and looking for work. She replied to an advertisement for employment at a bank, and was selected to go for an interview. After the interview, she decided to do some magical work to further her chances. The main image in this magical work was an intense visualization of herself being at work in the building, so this was quite easy.

Surprise, surprise! She did not get the job at the bank. However, a few days later a friend phoned her and said she had been offered a job as secretary at a small publishers, but had to refuse, and asked if our subject was interested.

She went to the interview and was given the post. And the punchline? The publishers were housed on the top floor of the same building the bank was in.

In the event, personal differences made it unpleasant to work there, and after two months she left by mutual agreement.

Merlin and Morgana sum up: 'To us, the ending of the story is illustrative of the momentum of magical work. Magical forces will seek any means to realize the objective, even if it is not in the best interests of the person concerned. Unless, of course, you are clever enough to make sure you only ask for what you really want, rather than for what you think you want. And finally, it is important to choose your magical aim with care; in this case, working in a building is NOT the same as working at a bank which is located at that building.'

There is one type of spell-working in which precise visualization is not necessary: the sending of a feeling of love, peace and reassurance. Merlin and Morgana cite the case of a 49-year-old woman who applied to them for help: she was overweight, looking 69, and depressed, and had made three suicide attempts. They were able to help her to begin with; then two simultaneous personal setbacks seemed to take her right back to square one. At this stage they concentrated their magical work's main aim ' ... to create a restful atmosphere around her, so that she could find the time to come to grips with herself again without being overwhelmed by problems outside herself. The magical work in this case was not very specified at all – more a question of sending out feelings and an atmosphere of love, peace, rest and quiet, than a clear image. We have found this to work quite well in many cases. Where specific images may lead to unintended results if you choose your image wrongly, a well-defined emotion may give fine, though equally unexpected, results.'

In this particular case, one effect was that both the woman's personal setbacks solved themselves within a week – and over a year later they had a happy postcard from her on holiday in Cornwall, whereas before she had been scared even to go outside her own front door.

It seems at times as though 'someone up there' has a wicked sense of humour when it comes to carelessly worded spells. There is the often-quoted occasion when Alex Sanders told his coven he wanted gold, and got them to work for it – and next morning somebody appeared on his doorstep and presented him with a bowl of goldfish. And Nigel Bourne tells us how he and Seldiy once worked a spell for a particular sum of money – and then went out into the street and found the exact amount scattered around in Monopoly money. 'Someone up there' must only have been having fun, because very soon afterwards the right amount of real money came to them.

Passionately expressed wishes can, of course, work as spells. Once, when we were even more broke than usual, Janet cried in exasperation; 'I wish we had half a million!' Not long afterwards our literary agent wrote to say she had sold one of Stewart's short stories to a magazine for half a million Italian lire – about £235 sterling. So if you are spell-working for money, specify the currency!

An amusing story of spell failure concerns Dr John Fian, one of the sixteenth-century North Berwick witches (see p. 148). Dr Fian was a schoolmaster of Saltpans, who fancied the sister of one of his pupils. He promised to teach him without whipping if he would bring him 'three hairs from his sister's privities'.

The boy shared a bed with his sister, and he tried to steal three of her pubic hairs while she was asleep; but the girl woke up and told their mother. The mother was herself a witch, so she suspected what lay behind the attempt – and after she had given him a thrashing, the boy confessed.

So the mother cut three hairs from the udder of a young heifer and told her son to give them to Dr Fian, pretending they came from his sister. The schoolmaster worked his love spell on them – and it succeeded, though certainly not as he expected. The heifer sought out Dr Fian, 'leaping and dancing upon him', and chased him through the town.

Having told that story at his expense, it is only fair to add that Dr Fian, at the 1590 trial, bore himself most bravely of all the seventy accused, refusing to confess under the cruellest torture. King James VI (later James I of England) watched his torturing and personally condemned him to death.

# XI  *Spells of the Ancient World*

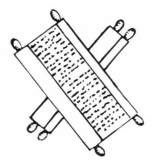

The Ancient Egyptians had an outstanding reputation for magic and spell-working. As Wallis Budge puts it (*Egyptian Magic*, p. 4): 'Hebrew, and Greek, and Roman writers referred to them as experts in the occult sciences, and as the possessors of powers which could, according to circumstances, be employed to do either good or harm to man.'

Moses and Aaron, it will be remembered, were Egyptian-trained; and the story of the rods and serpents, in which they beat the Egyptian magicians at their own game, is only one instance of their Egyptian-type magic. Their rods (magic wands) were used to turn water into blood, to conjure up frogs, lice, locusts and hail mixed with fire. Moses was also able to command the receding and returning of the sea – a power claimed by Egyptian magicians long before Moses, at least as far back as the time of the Great Pyramid.

The Koran describes Moses frankly, and correctly, as a magician.

The Egyptians used wax images in much the same way as later

European magicians – but one example is of particular interest, in that the image was not that of the individual concerned but of a kind of intermediary in a love spell. A man desiring a particular woman had to make an image of a dog from wax mixed with pitch, and engrave certain words of power on it. He would then stand the dog on a tablet, also engraved with words of power, and place both tablet and dog on a tripod. The man then had to recite both sets of words of power, and one of two things would happen. Either the dog-image would snarl and snap at the man, in which case he would not win the lady; or it would bark, in which case the lady would come to him.

(It may be argued, not unreasonably, that this was in fact a form of self-examination. If the man knew subconsciously that his desire for the lady was ill-advised, he would project this knowledge into belief that the dog had snarled. If he knew in his heart that the desired match held promise, he would believe the dog had barked. By no means an unhealthy approach to the problem.)

About 1100 BC ladies of the harem of Rameses III made wax images of him in an attempt to bring about his death.

Many of the texts in the Egyptian *Book of the Dead* (see Bibliography under Budge), which were inscribed on papyri interred with the deceased, were in effect spells to protect him or her against the perils of the journey into the afterlife. The deceased's great hope would be to journey through Heaven in the boat of the Sun god Ra, the Boat of a Million Years, so a picture of the boat would be drawn with special green ink on a piece of papyrus, with the figures of Isis, Thoth, Shu and Kephera, as well as the deceased, shown sailing in it. This papyrus would be blessed with words of power and fastened to the breast of the deceased but not actually touching the body.

The deceased's vital attributes would be protected by such papyrus spells as: 'Hail, thou god Tem, grant thou unto me the sweet breath which dwelleth in thy nostrils.... I keep watch over the Egg of the Great Cackler; I germinate as it germinateth; I live as it liveth; my breath is its breath.'

Egyptians had a strong belief in the magical power of words, whether written on papyrus, painted on walls, inscribed on amulets or talismans or spoken in the correct tones. And most powerful of all were the names of gods or goddesses. Egyptian thinking, certainly among the educated, knew perfectly well that there was only one ultimate Divine Source; their huge pantheon of deities represented faces or aspects of this Source, and (like thinking pagans today) they vividly personified these aspects and were meticulous about appealing to the appropriate one in any given situation.

Evil or dangerous factors were also personified and, where necessary, named and directly addressed in binding formulae. For example, a spell for protection against dangerous beasts: 'Hail, lord of the Gods! Drive away from me the lions of the country of Meru, and the crocodiles which come forth from the river, and the bites of all poisonous reptiles which crawl forth from their holes. Get thee back, O crocodile Mak, thou son of Set! Move not by means of thy tail! Work not thy legs and feet! Open not thy mouth! Let the water which is before thee turn into a consuming fire ...' and so on. These words were said over a picture of the god Amun painted on clay, with the crocodile Mak under his feet.

The Pharaoh Nectanebo II (c. 359–341 BC) had a great reputation as a magician, astrologer and diviner of the future. He used sympathetic magic to help his naval forces. He floated toy boats representing both sides, with miniature crews, in a huge bowl of water, uttered words of power to bring the tiny dolls to life and then used the miniature models to enact an Egyptian victory. He defended his land successfully for many years, but it is said that on the last occasion on which he used his bowl-of-water method, against a combined threat from the East, he saw to his dismay that the gods of Egypt were steering the invaders' miniature ships. Realizing that the gods had ordained that his reign was at an end, he dressed as a commoner and escaped to Pella in Macedonia, where he established himself as a physician and soothsayer. Egypt was overwhelmed first by the Persians and then by the Greek Ptolemies; Nectanebo was the last native ruler of Ancient Egypt.

Wax image-making would seem to be as old as magic itself. The Roman poet Ovid tells of the witch Medea: 'She puts a curse on the absent victims, and shapes waxen images, and sticks sharp pins into the wretched livers.' Ovid describes Medea's spells in great detail in his *Metamorphoses*.

Ovid again: 'Does my body languish, doomed by a Thessalian drug? Does a charm or herb injure me, wretch that I am? Or has a witch nailed down my name in Punic wax, or driven fine needles into my very liver?' (Thessaly had a strong reputation for witchcraft.)

The spells which Ovid reports make great use of the magic number three. 'Thrice she purifies the old man with flame, thrice with water, and thrice with sulphur .... Thrice she caressed him with her hand, thrice she uttered spells.'

The Roman poet Tibullus also emphasizes: 'Chant thrice, spit three times after uttering the incantations.'

Horace has his witch Candida use a wax image for love spells. Theocritus tells the same of his witch, Samaetha.

A Roman spell to banish pain, written on a piece of paper hung round the neck:

An ant has no blood nor bile;
Flee, uvula, lest a crab eat you.

Another Roman spell, to cure gout, was given by the author Varro
(116–27 BC). It must be done while fasting. One had to touch the
earth, spit downwards, and recite:

O Earth, keep the pain,
And health with me remain
In my feet.

Greece was another country with wax-image traditions. It is said that
Aristotle gave Alexander the Great a box with a number of wax figures
nailed into it face down, representing the various kinds of armed
forces Alexander might find himself facing. He must never let it out of
his hand, or the hand of a trusted servant. Whenever he picked it up
or put it down, he must recite certain words over it. The enemies the
figures represented would then be powerless to resist him.

According to the Greek historian Xenophon, the great philosopher
Socrates believed firmly in the power of spells. Asked if he 'knew such
arts', he replied: 'Through what other influences do you think that
Apollodorus and Antisthenes stay with me, and Cebes and Simias
come to me from Thebes? I do not accomplish this without many
love-charms, incantations and magic wheels.'

The Christmas custom of kissing under the mistletoe has its roots in
far more ancient spell-working. Doubtless because of its semen-like
juice, the mistletoe has always been a symbol of fertility. Pliny
particularly recommended mistletoe growing on an oak tree, for
women who wished to conceive to carry about with them.

Mistletoe was also regarded as a lock-picker. Albertus Magnus, the
thirteenth-century magician, wrote: 'This herb Misseltoe, with a
certain other herb, which is named Martegon, that is Silphion or
Laserpitium, as it is written in the Almans language, it openeth all
locks.' Another phallic overtone?

The pagan associations of mistletoe are so strong that it is still
forbidden to take it into a church in most parishes. An exception was
at York Minster in the Middle Ages, when a branch was always laid on
the altar from Christmas Eve until Twelfth Night.

In ancient Babylon, one destroyed a malignant spell by invoking the
fire god Gibil while burning a peeled onion and a crushed date.

An ancient Chinese spell inscribed on a sword: 'I wield the large sword of Heaven to cut down spectres in their live shapes; one stroke of this divine blade disperses a myriad of these beings.'

As we explain on p. 99, because of the pictorial nature of Chinese characters, written or inscribed words have always been regarded in China as being of great magical power.

The first-century AD Jewish magician Honi Ha Ma'agel is one of the earlier reported users of the Magic Circle. He would cast one and work within it to conjure up rain. He had such a reputation for this that he was known as 'the Circle-Drawer'.

A traditional Hebrew spell to banish fever took the name of the demon responsible and intoned it with repeated beheadings, thus:

> Ochnotinos
> Chnotinos
> Notinos
> Tinos
> Inos
> Nos
> Os

As the name disappeared, so did the fever.

This kind of diminishing-name incantation is also found in a positive sense – for example, in a Spanish-Moorish spell to secure a husband, which did the same with a local form of the name of Allah:

> Ojala
> Ojal
> Oja
> Oj
> O

In this case, the idea was not to weaken but to concentrate the power of the Name; it will be noticed that the word was not beheaded but reduced step by step to the single initial vowel which was regarded as its essence.

The word 'Abracadabra', often quoted as a synonym for, or to imply, 'mumbo-jumbo', was in fact also a diminishing-word spell, particularly against fever.

This pyramid-pattern can work both ways. A pair of modern examples from Valerie Worth's *The Crone's Book of Days*, (pp. 94–5); first a spell to decrease another's power:

To shrink his lust
And wither his dust,
Call the first,
Diminish the rest,
Whisper the last:

NORODAROGOR
RODAROGOR
DAROGOR
ROGOR
OGOR
OR

Second, to increase one's own power:

Lie down as dead,
Then upward waken;
Raise this word
Thy strength to quicken:

OR
ORON
DORON
RODORON
GORODORON
ROGORODORON

A different form of the letter-pattern spell is represented by the palindromic SATOR square:

SATOR
AREPO
TENET
OPERA
ROTAS

– used as a charm against disease and death by fire. It has a long and curious history, dating back at least to an example of it in the ruins of Pompeii. Leo Louis Martello devotes a whole interesting chapter to it in his *Witchcraft: The Old Religion*.

But to return to ancient spells in general. The Sanskrit magical text *Atharva Veda* gives a spell to acquire virility:

Thou art the plant which Varuna had dug up for him by Gandharva, thou potent and lusty herb, which we have uprooted.
 Ushas, Surya, Pragapati, all are with me; all will give me the potent

force I seek! O Indra, give this material power; it has heat like that of the
fire. Like the he-antelope, O Herb, thou hast all the force there is, as the
brother of the great Soma.

Varuna is a sky and water god; the Gandharvas are singers in the
Heaven of the battle and rain god Indra and have a fondness for
women; Ushas is the dawn goddess, Surya the Sun goddess, and
Pragapati the protector of those who beget offspring. Soma is the
nectar of the gods, and also a god himself, link between Heaven and
Earth.

The Koran gives a spell against evil sorcery: 'I take refuge with the
Lord of the Daybreak from the evil of the blowers upon Knots, and
from the evil of the envious one when he envies.'
   'Blowing upon knots' was a favourite Arabic method of
spell-working. The knots were tied in strings of multicoloured threads
and were not only used malevolently: they featured in spells to cure
illness or banish evil spells – though even this, of course, would be
frowned upon by Muslim orthodoxy. The Roman author Petronius
(time of Nero) also mentions the use of multicoloured threads to
banish an evil spell.
   Knot-tying has always been one method of achieving magical
concentration, and still is.

The sacred Persian texts *Avesta* give a spell against evil: 'Get thee a
feather of the wide-feathered bird Varenjana, O Spitama Zarathustra.
With that feather thou shalt rub thy body, with that feather thou shalt
curse back thine enemy. He who hath a bone of the mighty bird or a
feather of the mighty bird gaineth divine favour. No one, however
magnificent, smiteth him or turneth him to flight.'

Ancient Indian love spells tended to be quite uninhibited. Here is a
woman's incantation from the *Atharva Veda*: 'By the power and Laws
of Varuna I invoke the burning force of love, in thee, for thee. The
desire, the potent love-spirit which all the gods have created in the
waters, this I invoke, this I employ, to secure thy love for me! Indrani
has magnetized the waters with this love-force. And it is that, by
Varuna's laws, that I cause to burn! Thou wilt love me with a burning
desire.'
   Varuna is a sky and water god who maintains order in the universe.
His wife Varuni is the goddess of spirituous liquors, who was born of
the Churning of the Ocean (hence 'created in the waters'). Indrani
(whose name means 'of the senses') is the goddess of sensual pleasure,
the voluptuously beautiful wife of Indra.

It is worth remembering that seasonal rituals, which in one form or another must be as old as humankind, are themselves spells – sympathetic magic to help the Sun and Mother Earth to maintain their endless cycle of fertility and repose, withdrawal and revival. And these rituals have survived stubbornly throughout the ages, in everything from folk custom to the Christian calendar.

The rational view might appear to be that such sympathetic magic is no longer necessary, because, whatever our ancestors believed, we now know that it has no effect whatsoever on the rotation of the Earth, the tilt of its axis, and its orbiting round the Sun. True enough; but does not the real value of such rituals remain what it has always been – to work magic on ourselves, by putting ourselves intimately in tune with the cycle of Nature and the rhythms of Mother Earth?

And is that not more important than ever, now that urbanization, over-population and the by-products of industry have estranged us from those rhythms to the point of global danger? The point where (for example) the destruction of the tropical rain-forests, and the damage to the ozone layer, threatens to alter the Earth's weather patterns and the actual nature, all over the world, of the seasons we are talking about?

Ritually celebrating the milestones in those seasonal patterns can help us to understand, value and preserve them.

Rituals of the Winter Solstice are among the most deep-rooted and most fraught with intensity of feeling, because they mark what was to primitive mankind the most perilous time of all – when everything must be done to ensure the rebirth of the Sun, without which all would perish. Every culture and every religion – particularly in the northern latitudes where the extremes of summer and winter are most marked – has greeted suitably this nodal point in the year; and Christianity had to follow suit. The birth of Jesus, the great Palestinian teacher whom Christianity deified into its own Sun god, is undated in the New Testament and was at first celebrated at various times. But as late as AD 273 the Church fixed the birthday of 'the Sun of Righteousness' at the Winter Solstice so that, as St Chrysostom explained, ' ... while the heathen were busied with their profane rites, the Christians might perform their holy ones without disturbance'.

One Winter Solstice spell which millions observe, and which is entirely pagan, is the Christmas tree. This is pure sympathetic magic – taking an evergreen tree and loading it with symbolic blossoms and fruit to conjure back fertility.

The springtime fertility-spell significance of Easter eggs is self-evident (though what is seldom realized is that the word 'Easter' derives from Eostre, the Teutonic Earth-Mother goddess in her springtime Maid aspect).

Midsummer is still celebrated with bonfires in the west of Ireland and has been very loosely Christianized by attaching it to St John's Eve, 23 June; but it too (as we discovered when we lived there) is thoroughly pagan in spirit, a direct descendant of the fire festival which marked the zenith of the Sun's cycle. As such, it is celebratory rather than spell-working, but the spell factor survives in the custom of driving cattle between two fires to ensure their health and productivity – a custom also found at that other great fire festival, Beltane (Gaelic Bealtaine) or May Eve.

We could fill pages with the magical significance of these and the other festivals of Imbolg (Candlemas, 2 February), Lughnasadh (harvest, 31 July) and Samhain (Hallowe'en, 31 October), not to mention the two Equinoxes, but we have covered these in depth in our *Eight Sabbats for Witches*, and we hope we have said enough here to make our point.

# XII   *Spells of the Middle Ages and Later*

Medieval spells can be studied from two main sources. First, the spells used by ordinary people, and by grass-roots witches, have come down to us via folklore, the fiction and drama of the time, and the records of the witch trials – these trial records, of course, being subject to much distortion (if a defendant referred to a pagan god, for example, she would be recorded as referring to the Devil) and often consisting of statements made under torture. So the evidence we have on grass-roots medieval spell-working is all second-hand at the very least.

The second source is first-hand – from the grimoires or 'grammars' of ritual magicians.

The most famous and influential of these grimoires is *The Key of Solomon*, or, by its full title, *Clavicula Salomonis, the Key of Solomon the King*. The first known mention of *Clavicula Salomonis* is in a pamphlet of 1456. Various versions of it exist, many of them as Latin, French or Italian manuscripts (claiming to have been translated from the Hebrew) in the British Museum. It was from these BM manuscripts that MacGregor Mathers edited the first English translation, which he published in 1888. The currently available edition of the Mathers translation was published by Routledge & Kegan Paul in 1972, with a foreword by Richard Cavendish. Page references given below are to this edition.

Mathers himself (p. viii) saw 'no reason to doubt' the tradition that the *Key* was originally the work of King Solomon. But as Cavendish points out (p. v): 'That luxurious monarch of the tenth century BC was renowned for his wisdom and for his unhealthy interest in foreign women and heathen gods, but he is unlikely to have shared the *Key*'s concern with demons who inhabit a hell of much later date.'

Of these, the *Key* has plenty. In fact, the whole work (like most of the medieval grimoires) uses Christian terminology throughout and maintains that the magician's power comes from God, even when he is working for destruction, death ' ... or "for preparing powders provocative of madness" or for other purposes of less than heavenly morality" (Cavendish, p. v). Demons and angels alike are summoned and ordered to carry out the magician's commands, just as Solomon was said to have conscripted legions of demons, bound by the power of his God-given magic ring, to help build the Jerusalem Temple.

The Babylonians and later the Arabs held the same view – that, since demons were less powerful than God, if one knew the correct Words of Power, one could command them to work, even if unwillingly for constructive ends. (Summoned demons were commanded at least to look respectable, according to the *Key*. In one potent conjuration (p. 30) the magician orders them, by a long list of Names of God: 'Come ye at once without any hideousness or deformity before us, come ye without monstrous appearance, in a gracious form or figure.')

There are several spells in the *Key*, each preceded by lengthy conjurations calling on God and various spirits. Typical (p. 49) is one to discover who has committed a theft. A sieve is suspended by a cord 'wherewith a man has been hung', with certain signs written in blood inside its rim. Under this is placed a brass bowl of fountain water, and the words '*Dies mies yes-chet bene done fet Donnima Metemauz*' are uttered. The sieve is then spun with the left hand, and the water in the bowl swirled in the opposite direction with a twig of green laurel in the right hand. Sieve and water are then left to settle, and when both are still, the magician must gaze fixedly in the water, where he will see the face of the thief. To make sure he will recognize him in the flesh, he then marks this image with his Magical Sword, and ' ... that sign which thou shalt have cut therewith in the water, shall be really found thereafter upon his own person.'

An invisibility spell (p. 52) involves detailed instructions for the making and inscribing of a yellow wax image of a man, which you carry in your left pocket, telling it, 'Come unto me and never quit me whithersoever I shall go', whenever you wish to go somewhere without being seen.

Animal rights activists might approve of the spell which immediately follows this one, 'To Hinder a Sportsman from Killing any Game', but for the fact that it involves writing magical characters with the blood of a black hen on the skin of a hare.

Other *Key* spells are for becoming master of 'a Treasure possessed by the Spirits', for seeking favour and love and for 'operations of Mockery, Invisibility and Deceit'.

The *Key* gives a procedure (p. 55) for making a carpet, woven of new white wool during the full Moon, into a magic one; not the Arabian Nights kind for flying but a carpet on which one sits to produce oracular utterances. The invocation runs: 'Agla, Agla, Agla, Agla! O Almighty God, Thou art the Life of the Universe, and rulest over the four parts of that immense area, through the power of Thy Holy Name Tetragrammaton: Yod, He, Vau, He! Bless this carpet in Thy name, as thou blessed the cloak of Elijah in the hands of Elijah; so that with Thy wings, I may be able to be protected against all; He shall hide thee under His wings and under His feathers thou shalt trust, and His truth shall be thy protection.' Tetragrammaton (Greek for 'four-letter') is the Name of God as a Cabalistic formula – the consonants of the secret Name the whole of which could be pronounced only once a year by the High Priest in the Holy of Holies of the Temple of Jerusalem. Attempts to vocalize it have produced the names Yahweh and Jehovah.

Certain elements in *The Key of Solomon* undoubtedly influenced the rituals of that important magical fraternity, the Order of the Golden Dawn, of which Mathers himself was leader at the turn of the century (though later deposed because of his tyrannical tendencies).

The authenticity of some allegedly ancient grimoires – such as the *Grimoire of Honorius the Great* (supposedly written by Pope Honorius III and condemned by Catholic writers as a forgery), the *Grimorium Verum* (said to have been published by Alibeck the Egyptian at Memphis in 1517) and the *Secret Grimoire of Turiel* (sold to Marius Malchus by an unfrocked priest in Las Palmas in 1927 – is much more questionable. On the first two and others, Idries Shah's *The Secret Lore of Magic* is worth reading.

However, here are one or two spells from genuine medieval writers. The thirteenth-century magician Albertus Magnus gave this incantation for banishing sickness:

*Ofano, Oblamo, Ospergo.*

*Hola Noa Massa.*
*Light, Beff, Cletemati, Adonai,*
*Cleona, Florit.*
*Pax Sax Sarax.*
*Afa Afca Nostra.*
*Cerum, Heaium, Lada Frium.*

And even more cryptically mysterious, three spells from Johann Weyer in his *De Praestigiis et Incantationibus ac Veneficiis* (1568). First, a charm to cure toothache: '*Galbex, galbat, galdes, galdat.*' And for protection against hydrophobia, a piece of bread inscribed with these words:

*Irioni khirioni, effer*
*Khuder fere.*

Or to cure hydrophobia, a piece of apple inscribed with:

*Hax, pax, max,*
*Deus adimax.*

(We hope it doesn't need emphasizing, these days, that if hydrophobia – rabies – is met or suspected, the police and medical services should be contacted, but fast; and spell-working should concentrate on supporting their efforts.)

Let us look now at the other end of the scale, and see what can be found of grass-roots and witch spell-working in the Middle Ages.

Shakespeare lived and wrote just after what is generally regarded as the Middle Ages, but the traditions we are considering were still very much alive; so his three witches in *Macbeth* can fairly be considered an outstanding example of the image of witchcraft in the drama or literature of the time.

On the face of it, apart from the high quality of his writing, they are conventional stereotypes. One of them boasts of killing livestock. The ingredients of their famous 'fillet of a fenny snake' magical brew, with its gruesome animal and human items, reflect this – though one should remember that many such formulae were often codes for ingredients less horrendous, to frighten off the inquisitive. For example, 'tongue of dog' and 'adder's fork' are simply the herbs hound's tongue (Cynoglossum) and adder's tongue (Ophioglossum), much used against dog- and snake-bites respectively.

But there are hints that Shakespeare may have had a picture of country witchcraft clearer than that propagated by the official persecutors. The latter were not, for example, interested in goddesses; they were out to prove allegiance to Satan. Yet there is no mention of Satan as lord of Shakespeare's three. Their mistress, who came and rebuked them because

> ... all you have done
> Hath been but for a wayward son
> Spiteful and wrathful; who, as others do,
> Loves for his own ends, not for you

was Hecate, Goddess of Witches.

They are credited with being able to conjure up winds and with the power to become invisible (Shakespeare's stage directions always say '*Exeunt ...*' for ordinary mortals, but for these three every time it is 'Witches vanish').

And with divination – dramatized as the ability to conjure up apparitions, but the principle is the same. Next time they meet the 'wayward son' after Hecate's reprimand, they present him with truthful predictions which have catches in them. What he makes of these is up to him. If his ambition and tunnel-vision make him interpret the predictions his own way and fail to understand the warnings, the results will be on his own head. Every clairvoyant, Tarot reader or divinator has met clients like that.

Shakespeare also refers, in *A Midsummer Night's Dream* to shape-changing. Puck speaks of the occasions

> When I a fat and bean-fed horse beguile,
> Neighing in likeness of a filly-foal;
> And sometimes lurk I in a gossip's bowl
> In very likeness of a roasted crab,
> And, when she drinks, against her lips I bob,
> And on her withered dewlap pour the ale.
> The wisest aunt, telling the saddest tale,
> Sometime for three-foot stool mistaketh me;
> Then slip I from her bum, down topples she ....

Shakespeare's contemporary, Ben Jonson, incidentally, also put into verse the coming-together of witches, in his *Three Witches' Charms*:

> Dame, dame! the watch is set:
> Quickly come, we are all met.
> From the lakes and from the fens,
> From the rocks and from the dens,

From the woods and from the caves,
From the churchyards, from the graves,
From the dungeon, from the tree
That they die on, here are we!
    Come she not yet?
    Strike another heat!


On the question of invisibility spells, such as *The Key of Solomon* one quoted above, many reports from witnesses at witch trials will, of course, have been simply made up to imply that the accused was present at the crime even though nobody saw him or her. But what about invisibility spells which were practised and believed in by the spell-worker?

Some of these may have been hypnotic, to convince the people concerned that they could not see somebody who was, in fact, physically there; any competent hypnotist can do that today, though whether some psychically powerful spell-workers can do it on a telepathic level is another question.

But most of these spells would actually have been to achieve unnoticeability rather than invisibility (on the principle that the best place to hide a needle is not in a haystack but in a needle factory). Such a spell would affect the worker's own behaviour and attitude to this end, rather than other people's.

Invisibility spells are many and various, but we have come across only one inaudibility spell. In Scottish Highland clan warfare, it used to be believed that, when an attack was planned, the chief could take a sprig of churchyard yew in his left hand and denounce the enemy – who would then be unable to hear him, although everyone else could. The attackers would thus have the advantage of surprise but could claim afterwards that fair warning was loudly and clearly given!

An alternative to being invisible to others is to send them to sleep, and for this the gruesome device known as the Hand of Glory is referred to in witch trials. It was the hand of a hanged man, squeezed dry of blood and pickled for two weeks with salt, saltpetre and long peppers. It was then parched in the sun or dried in an oven with vervain and fern. Candles would then be attached to the fingers – candles made, according to one recipe, from the fat of a hanged man, virgin wax and Lapland sesame. It was said that when these finger-candles were lit, a thief could take the Hand into a house and all its occupants would fall asleep while he robbed it at his leisure. (A similar belief used to be held in Ireland – that if lit candles were put in the hand of a corpse during a wake, all the mourners would fall asleep, and the house could be robbed.)

At other trials, it was claimed that, while the candles of a Hand of Glory were burning, witches could work powerful malevolent magic.

The magical value of the hand of a hanged man was extended to the rope which hanged him: it was supposed to have healing powers – for example, for headaches, if a piece of it was worn round the head or in the hat; in Russia, a piece was carried in the pocket for luck in gambling. Hangmen used to make useful side-profits from selling pieces of such ropes.

A dead hand did not have to belong to an executed felon or a suicide to be curative, though these two kinds were the most powerful. Stroking the affected part with the hand of an ordinary corpse was believed to be effective. In Cornwall, after such therapeutic stroking, one dropped the bandage which had covered the injury on the coffin during the burial service; but the cure would work only if the corpse was not that of a near relative. In some places, a dead man's hand was needed to cure a woman, and vice versa.

Even something which had been in touch with a corpse's hand – such as a ring taken from it, or a piece of bread and butter which had been laid on it – was believed to carry a healing charge.

To return to the living body. Hair has always been regarded as magically powerful. The biblical story of Samson and Delilah enshrines this ancient belief, though women's hair was believed to be even more powerful than men's.

In the persecution days, suspected witches were often shaved of all body hair to deprive them of their magical powers. In several cases it was claimed that women who had stubbornly refused to confess suddenly admitted everything once their body hair had been removed.

Arnold and Patricia Crowther devoted a whole interesting chapter to the subject in their book *The Secrets of Ancient Witchcraft* (see Bibliography). They cited (p. 32) one twentieth-century case from Spain, of a woman who went to a reputed witch because her husband was being unfaithful. The witch was willing to prepare a love charm, for which she required some of the woman's armpit hair. She was unable to supply it because she always shaved her armpits.

The witch was horrified and told her, 'I can do nothing more for you. Come back to me when your hair has grown again. Your stupid act has probably lost you your husband.'

The woman was sceptical but did as she was told, coming back two months later with the necessary hair. Her husband returned to her and never strayed again.

Australian Aborigine witch-doctors tie women's hair to their death-pointing bones, believing that it is the hair which is the source of power, the bone being a mere vehicle for it.

In some countries, witches dye their pubic hair bright red to increase their power to scare away evil spirits.

This concept overlaps the belief that demons and ghosts are frightened by exposed genitals – a belief shared by some Christians. Martin Luther, tormented by nightly visions of Satan, exposed his genitals and buttocks to exorcise him. And this would appear to be the explanation of the surprising carvings to be found on many medieval churches, known as Sheila-na-gigs, squatting naked female figures displaying exaggerated genitals. Their purpose was to discourage evil spirits from invading the holy ground.

Demons' and ghosts' aversion to exposed genitals was often said to extend to the naked body as a whole; and the Crowthers (*ibid.*, p. 35) suggest that this may be one of the roots of ritual nudity. 'One of the reasons that witches work naked in the circle is to keep evil entities away, and rituals performed in the nude 'are freer from troublesome elementals than those performed in robes or some other form of dress.'

One accusation much levelled by the medieval persecutors was that witches celebrated the Black Mass, a blasphemous and blatantly sexual travesty of the Catholic Mass, but this was pure invention.

As Rossell Hope Robbins puts it (*The Encyclopaedia of Witchcraft and Demonology*, p. 50), ' ... the black mass, as something that historically occurred, is one of the biggest intellectual frauds ever imposed on the lay public. It was only natural that the inquisitors and the lay witch hunters who aped them would think of witchcraft in inverse terms to the religion they knew; witchcraft was made a conscious parody of Christianity.'

In fact, amatory (i.e., love-spell) masses had long been an accepted, if to modern thinking bizarre, feature of orthodox Church practice; and by the seventeenth century nobles of the French Court, without any secrecy, hired fifty or sixty priests to conduct unashamedly erotic masses for magical purposes. These, and mortuary masses to bring death to somebody, were not regarded as heretical and at most resulted in the banishment of the laymen and priests involved.

Not until the nineteenth century, Robbins points out (*ibid.*, p. 51), ' ... did a few wayward minds create the black mass as it is thought of today, a service dedicated to anti-Christ, or a supposed relic of anti-Christian folklore'.

It was not only malevolent witchcraft that the persecutors condemned. For example, the Channel Island of Jersey in 1591 passed an ordinance forbidding people to seek 'assistance from witches and diviners in their ills and afflictions' on pain of one month's imprisonment on bread and water.

English civil law in the Middle Ages did not itself condemn benevolent sorcery – i.e., magic worked for such purposes as healing – but from 900 onwards ecclesiastical law punished all magical working, including curative, with excommunication, and those found guilty were handed over to the civil authorities for execution.

The official view came to prevail that white witches were as much to be condemned as black, because both drew their power from the Devil. So, if anything, the benevolent and healing spell-worker was more dangerous than the malignant one, being more likely to lead the innocent into error.

As the Puritan writer William Perkins declared in 1608: 'Though the witch were in many respects profitable, and did not hurt, but procured much good, yet because he hath renounced God, his king and governor, and hath bound himself by other laws to the service of the enemies of God and his Church, death is his portion justly assigned him by God; he may not live.'

The report of the witch trial of Ursula Kemp at St Osyth in 1582 includes what sounds like a reasonably accurate account of a healing spell for arthritis which a wisewoman had given her. She had to ' ... take hog's dung and charnell and put them together and hold them in her left hand, and to take in the other hand a knife, and to prick the medicine three times, and then cast the same into the fire, and to take the said knife, and to make three pricks under a table, and to let the knife stick there. And after that to take three leaves of sage, and as much of herb John (alias herb grace) and put them into ale, and drink it last at night and first in the morning; and that she taking the same had ease of her lameness.'

Ursula Kemp was condemned and executed.

On the malevolent side, the trial of the sisters Margaret and Philippa Flower at Lincoln in 1618 concerned the killing of Henry, Lord Rosse, son of the Earl of Rutland (from whose service they had been dismissed), by the use of an item of his personal property, and also involved a cat familiar.

Philippa confessed that she ' ... brought from the Castle the right-hand glove of Lord Henry Rosse, which she delivered to her mother, who presently rubbed it on the back of her spirit Rutterkin; and then put it into hot boiling water. Afterward she pricked it often and buried it in the yard, wishing the Lord Rosse might never thrive. And so her sister Margaret continued with her mother, where she often saw the cat, Rutterkin, leap on her shoulder and suck her neck.'

This last item was typical. Witches were supposed to have familiars, usually taking the form of domestic animal pets but being in fact demons, whom they suckled at nipples (which Satan had given them) hidden in various parts of their bodies. The search for these 'witches' marks' was a regular feature of the examination of the accused, and many a woman's fate was sealed by the discovery of a perfectly natural mole, wart or other blemish.

In Finland, to which Christianity did not come till 1157, persecution of witches never reached the level of hysteria and cruelty it did in most countries of Europe, except for a brief flare-up in one area under Swedish influence. Witchcraft and sorcery were condemned by law, but within its own terms that law was sensibly and calmly applied. Only *maleficia* – spell working to do harm – was punishable by death; prophesying and such pagan practices as sacrificing to trees merely incurred fines.

A typical attitude was that of Bishop Fsak Rothovius, preaching at Turku University in 1640: 'When people fall ill, they seek help from the devil by laying wax figures, candles, squirrel skins and other things on the altar, and on certain days sacrifice sheep and goats' – but such healing methods he regretted as superstition, not as heresy.

Finnish witches had the reputation of selling winds to sailors, as we shall see on p. 148.

In Europe in general, healing spells and incantations were permissible, apparently, as long as they were expressed in Christian terms. A fifteenth-century English example, to stop bleeding: 'When our Lord Jesus Christ was done on the cross, then Longius came with his spear and pierced him in the side. Blood and water came out at the wound. Longius wiped his eyes and saw a man through the holy virtue that God showed there. I conjure thee, blood, that thou come not out of this Christian man.'

Such incantations were not acceptable in all countries of Europe. In Norway in 1670, Ole and Lisbet Nypen were charged with using healing charms and incantations, one of which was to cure grippe: 'Christ walked to the church with a book in his hand. Came the Virgin Mary herself walking. "Why are you so pale, my blessed son?" "I have caught a powerful grippe." "I cure you of powerful grippe – cough grippe, intestinal grippe, back grippe, chest grippe – from flesh and bone, to beach and stone, in the name of the Father, Son, and Holy Ghost."

The Nypens were condemned on four counts, foremost of which was taking the Lord's name in vain, and were condemned to be burned.

Even St Thomas Aquinas gave grudging approval to talismans and amulets: 'To attach holy words about the neck, provided they contain nothing false or suspect, is certainly not unlawful, although it would be better to refrain.'

Scotland was less tolerant; there, the use of charms was punishable by burning to death.

Kramer and Sprenger's *Malleus Maleficarum* (1486; see Biblio-graphy under Kramer), the notorious handbook for witch persecutors, specified exactly what constituted a permissible charm. It must contain:

1.   No suggestion in the wording of any pact with the Devil (and no such intention by the user).

2.   No unknown names.

3.   No untruths.

4.   No ritual other than the Sign of the Cross.

5.   No belief in the power of the manner of writing, wearing or using the charm.

6.   Only biblical quotations in their original context.

7.   Affirmations that the effectiveness of the charm depended entirely upon the will of God.

These clauses – in particular 2, 3 and 5, and the parenthesis in 1 – would seem to have left plenty of scope for the judges' interpretation.

In England, incidentally, casting the horoscope of a monarch (except, of course, by royal command and confidentially) was defined as high treason, because enemies could make use of its unfavourable aspects.

Of the estimated 10 million people executed throughout Europe during the witch persecution, about ninety per cent were women, and *Malleus Maleficarum* must certainly bear its share of the blame for this. For a start, the title means *Hammer of the Witches* – and the word *maleficarum* ('of the witches') is feminine in gender; and throughout a witch is referred to as 'she'. Here is the book's opinion of women: 'What else is a woman but a foe to friendship, an unescapable punishment, a necessary evil, a natural temptation ... a domestic danger, painted with fair colours.... The first woman ... was formed from a bent rib.... And since through this defect she is an imperfect animal, she always deceives.' The authors even claimed that the word *femina* came from *fe*, faith, and *minus* – thus meaning 'lacking in faith'!

To end this chapter, let us look at one of the most famous witch trials of all, that of Isobel Gowdie in Scotland in 1662, which has more interesting elements than most.

It is open to many interpretations: at the one extreme, that her four separate confessions (made apparently without torture) were pure fantasy; and at the other, that she was reporting, albeit via her own vivid and credulous imagination, the activities and structure of an actual coven.

Robbins (*ibid.*, p. 232) says that she ' ... appeared clearly demented, although by her statements it is plain she believed what she confessed, no matter how impossible (such as turning herself into a jackdaw or a cat, and flying through the air to a sabbat)'.

Modern witches and occultists may well consider the possibility that Isobel and her judges, in all sincerity, were thinking in two different languages; they in terms of literal, physical truth, and she in terms of genuine, and deliberately sought, psychic experiences (which are by no means the same thing as dementia).

Isobel said she belonged to a coven of thirteen, led by 'the devil'. The judges, of course, would identify this figure with Satan; but there is much evidence that witches used it to describe the male leader of a coven – the word either deriving from the same much older etymological root as '*Deus*' or 'divine', or being used as a deliberate rejection of the Church rather than as a sign of allegiance to evil.

It must never be forgotten that witches were in danger of their lives. Covens would make quite sure that new initiates were left in no doubt that they had burned their Christian bridges behind them and that reversion and betrayal would mean condemning themselves as well as their fellows.

The coven leader (who in those days was usually, though not always, male) would be regarded by the members as representative of the God. He is variously described as being disguised as an animal, as a black man or as a man dressed in black. On this subject, see Margaret Murray's *The Witch-cult in Western Europe*, Chapter II.

Isobel's 'devil' was clearly a man. He initiated her, she said, in the church at Auldearne in 1647; when she denied her Christian baptism and he rebaptized her in her own blood which he sucked from her. (He also gave her the witch name of Janet!) He ruled his coven firmly, beating them with cords when their work failed to reach the standards he demanded or if they missed a coven meeting.

Isobel claimed that, when she went to a sabbat, she would leave a broom or a stool in the bed to delude her husband. One wonders if he was really deluded or simply got the message and knew when to ask no questions.

One very genuine-sounding element in Isobel's testimony is her constant quoting of verse-jingles used in spells. For example, the coven would raise a wind by beating a stone with a wet rag and chanting:

> I knock this rag upon this stone
> To raise this wind in the Devil's name;
> It shall not lie, until I please again.

Or for a shape-changing spell:

> I shall go into a hare,

> With sorrow and sigh and mickle care;
> And I shall go in the Devil's name
> Ay while I come home again.

Which would be reversed by:

> Hare, hare, God send thee care.
> I am in a hare's likeness just now.
> But I shall be in a woman's likeness even now.

The record of Isobel Gowdie's trial does not give the verdict or the sentence, but in the Scottish atmosphere of the time there can be little doubt about her fate. And while in England people condemned as witches were hanged, in Scotland they were burned at the stake.

# XIII  *Spells from Other Lands*

Michel Raoult, a Breton friend at present stationed in Africa, sends us an interesting spell from Burundi, for escaping from a pursuing enemy. As you run, you throw behind you, over your shoulder, first an egg, then a pebble and finally a broom. The egg will turn into a pool, the pebble into a mountain, and the broom into a thicket of thorns, which should be enough to deter him. Moral: never go out without your escape-kit of egg, pebble and broom!

We cannot resist adding a Breton spell which Michel has passed to us:

> *Deuit ganin-me da gompezenn al Levenez*
> *O! Mar goufec'h e teufec'h 'vit atao!*

Not a human spell but an incantation by one of the *femmes du Sid* (fairy women). It means:

Come with me to the plain of Joy.
Oh! If you knew, you would come there forever!

If you hear it, beware; she is trying to enchant you away to the Land of Eternal Youth (which the Gaels call *Tir na nÓg*), and if you succumb, you will never be seen in the ordinary world again. By all reports, though, it might be well worth it.

Diana from the Netherlands sends us a Dutch spell to get rid of hiccups. Translated, it runs:

I have the hic,
I have the swallow.
I give it to someone else
Who can cope with it.

'Children often use this spell, saying it gradually faster and faster,' she tells us.
(Not unlike the English spell of 'buying' a wart. You cure someone else's wart by buying it for a penny. You then cut a potato in half, your patient sticks the penny in his half, and you bury your half – (the wart being disposed of with it. It is surprising how often this works.)

Voodoo spells do not often surface in Britain, but while we were still living in London we did come across one interesting case.
A Jamaican and his white wife had a couple of lovely children and were a very happy family. But then a West Indian woman set her sights on the husband – not, it was clear, out of genuine love but because he was in a well-paid job and good-looking. Gradually the husband became lethargic and unwell, and in general not himself. The wife, who was psychically sensitive, felt that there was something strange happening. Then suddenly, and quite out of character, the husband told her he was leaving her for the other woman.
The wife kept her cool and asked the advice of a West Indian woman friend. The friend advised her to examine the garden around their house. She did so, and found a circle of rock salt and cigar butts, which she reported to her friend. The friend at once got in touch with an old lady of her family in Jamaica, who said what the wife should do.
So the wife, following this advice, gathered up all the rock salt and cigar butts she could find in the garden and mixed them with more rock salt which she bought herself. She had also been told to buy some good-quality cigars and to get some black cockerel feathers; these she managed to obtain from her butcher, on the excuse that she needed them for a costume.

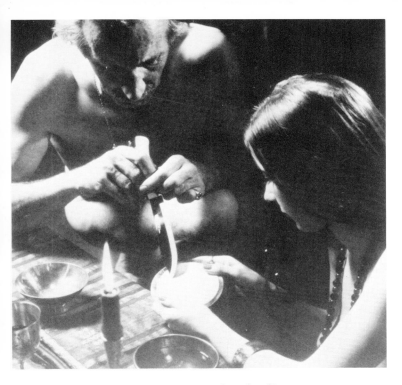

Consecrating a completed talisman

Working a needle spell of Venus

A Maori Tiki fertility
talisman, foetal in form

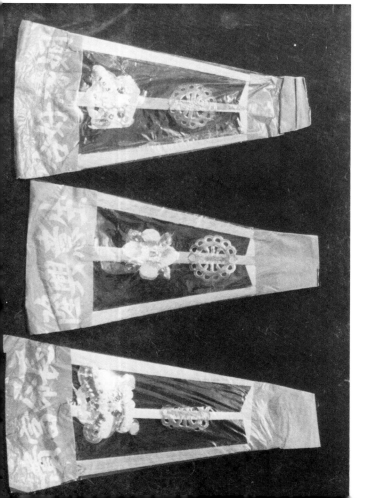

Chinese temple papers,
for burning to activate a
wish

Binding an image to neutralize malevolent working

Picking St John's Wort at Midsummer is a folk custom to ensure pregnancy

Dame Alice Kyteler's
fourteenth-century house in
Kilkenny, now an inn

Only smiths and farriers,
traditionally natural magicians,
may display a horseshoe
points downwards

The cottage of Biddy Early,
nineteenth-century wisewoman of
County Clare

Then she had to go, at midnight, and hide in the garden of the woman who was after her husband, and smoke the cigars. She felt both foolish and (being a non-smoker) slightly sick, but she stuck to her orders. She shredded her own cigar butts and added them to the mixture, which she then scattered widdershins (anti-clockwise) in a complete circle round the woman's house, and hid the cockerel feathers as near as possible to the front and back doors. All this involved some climbing over other people's walls to reach the back, in constant fear of being discovered, but she managed it safely and went home.

It worked. The woman suddenly lost interest in the husband, who was rapidly his former happy and loving self again.

Stanislao and Rosa of Miami, who run the Church of the Seven African Powers and organize correspondence courses on Santeria voodoo worship and magic, sent us a rather complicated spell which they say can be used for love or money, both of which come under the patronage of Ochun (Oshun), a Brazilian voodoo love-and-happiness goddess of Nigerian origin.

For this spell or 'ebbo' you need a medium-sized pumpkin (a vegetable associated with Ochun), honey, cloves, cinnamon sticks, river water, almond oil, five egg yolks, five floating candle-wicks, three brand-new needles, a square of yellow paper, five pennies and an image or picture of La Caridad del Cobre, Lady of Charity of Copper, patron saint of Cuba, who is identified with Ochun.

(Voodoo worshippers are quite uninhibited about identifying Catholic saints, from the Virgin Mary downwards, with their deities. This syncretism originally arose when Africans brought to America had to conceal their religion; concealment is no longer necessary, but the syncretism has become a habit, and they are quite happy with such interchangeability of symbols.)

Cut off the top of the pumpkin, but do not damage the sides. Empty out its contents. On a Saturday (Ochun's day), gather all your ingredients and place the pumpkin on a large white plate in front of the image of La Caridad.

If your request is for money, write it on the yellow paper; if it is for love, write the desired one's name. In either case, we are instructed, 'Make sure that your request is reasonable and not outlandish.' Pierce the name or the request with the three new needles, and put it in the bottom of the pumpkin.

Now add the five egg yolks, without breaking them, and place one whole clove, one cinnamon stick and finally one penny on top of each. Next, carefully pour in river water till the pumpkin is one-third full, and then pour almond oil on top of the water till it is half full. (That is, if you can afford that much almond oil on this side of the Atlantic!)

Float the five wicks on the almond oil and light them; and now voice your request to Ochen out loud.

The wicks must burn for five days continuously (five being Ochun's number). If one of them goes out, replace it with another wick. 'If they all go out,' the instructions warn, 'Ochun is trying to tell you something.'

When the fifth day is over, you throw the pumpkin and all its contents into a river, asking her blessing. And a final admonition: 'Do not make promises lightly to Ochun, as she is easily offended.'

Carole Pedley Chui, a Yorkshirewoman married to a Chinese, is a lawyer practising in Hong Kong, and a senior lecturer at its City Polytechnic. She tells us: 'I know I'm a witch and always was', so she has studied the magic of her adopted country with interest.

Hong Kong, because it missed the Cultural Revolution, has preserved much of the 'superstition' which the Mainland has ruthlessly tried to root out. I find it difficult to put my finger on the odd mixture of the supernatural and the businesslike in the Chinese outlook.

For instance, I read Tarot cards and I have a friend who is a full-time astrologer. We both find that Westerners – and Westernized Chinese – want to know about love and spirituality. The local Chinese want to know about money. 'When will I meet my rich man?' asks MiMi, my cousin-in-law. The answer is that she will get rich only through her own efforts, but she does not like that at all.

Whenever a new building is opened in Hong Kong, the *Feng Shui* man has to be called. This was true of the first Marks & Spencers store, which had to put in a tank of goldfish. *Feng* (or *Fung*) *Shui* means literally 'wind-water'. Chinese geomancy has a basis in clearly practical matters, such as airflow; but it also has more fanciful (it seems) aspects such as dragons in the earth. To sit well with the dragon is good, but to tease it by twitching its tail invites ruin.

This pervades all Hong Kong, though many will say they don't really believe in it. There has been hot debate about the new China Bank building's bad *Feng Shui* (mainlanders don't bring in the Feng Shui man, of course). The Hong Kong & Shanghai Bank, on the other hand, used the *Feng Shui* man, particularly to tell them where to site the bronze lions from the old building.

On protective spells – if a householder finds, say, an elevated roadway outside his window (happens all the time here!) or is told that the view of a chimney or a sharply angled roof is spoiling his luck, he will hang a *baat gwa* (eight-sided mirror) to reflect back the bad luck on its origin.

A friend who moved into a flat where someone had died was disconcerted to find a *baat gwa* on the neighbour's balcony, aimed at her, to deflect the bad luck coming from her flat.

One very popular form of good-luck spell is temple papers, which can be bought everywhere. 'Each has handwritten calligraphy, gold on red for good fortune, expressing, with all the pithiness the Chinese language is capable of, some good fate that is desired.'

Chinese writing is very condensed, and its appearance is regarded as being as important as its literal meaning; when choosing a name for a child, for instance, the look of that name on paper is a serious consideration. So, in a sense, as Carole points out, these temple papers are a combination of spell and talisman. Having bought the appropriate temple paper, you burn it to activate the wish. The sticks are sandalwood.

'In fact, burnt offerings are very Chinese. When someone dies, you go to the paper shop and buy paper money, paper houses, cars, yachts, whatever, and burn them for the person's use in the afterlife. The afterlife is depressingly like Hong Kong life at the moment – all competition, and who has the most status symbols, I fear. These temple blessings are bought from the same people who make the paper offerings. And the paper offerings are so beautifully hand-made, with calligraphy, that it seems a shame to burn them.'

Carole sent us three different temple papers, which you will see in the Plates section.

The Finnish national epic *Kalevala* incorporates much folklore – among it the two following magical incantations. First, against sickness in general:

> Sickness, vanish into the sky!
> Pain, fly up into the air.
> Burning vapour, rise up into the air!
> So that the wind may take thee away.
> So that the storm may chase thee to far places
> Where neither Sun nor Moon gives light,
> Where no hot wind burns the flesh.

The second is an incantation to stop a flow of blood:

> Hear, O blood! Instead of flowing,
> Instead of pouring out in a warm flood,
> O blood, stop like a wall;
> Like a hedge;
> Like a reef in the ocean,
> Like a stiff reed on the moors,
> Like a rock in a field,
> A pine-tree in the forest.

The Cherokee Indian shamans have an incantation to cure cripples:

> You, O Red Woman, you have caused it. You have put the
> intruder under him.
> Ha! Now you have come from the Sun Land. You have
> brought the small red seats with your feet resting upon them.
> Ha! Now they have swiftly moved away from you. Relief is
> accomplished.

A Malay spell to cure fever requires seven cigarettes, seven betel leaf chews, seven bananas, parched rice and an egg. All these must be rolled up in banana leaf and left at a three-way crossroads, with the incantation:

> Jembalang Jembali, Demon of the Earth,
> Accept this portion as your payment
> And restore [name].
> But if you do not restore him,
> I shall curse you with the saying
> 'There is no god but God.'

A Malayan invocation for summoning a wind addresses it respectfully:

> Come hither, Sir, come hither, my Lord,
> Let down your locks so long and flowing.

In the Gilbert Islands of Polynesia, the power to work weather magic seems to be an *ex officio* matter. Retired British colonial officer Arthur Grimble, in his fascinating book *Return to the Islands* (see Bibliography), wrote: 'My adoption way back in 1918, into the Tarawa sect of the royal and priestly clan of Karongoa had given me the right to practise the magic of rain-making and rain-dismissing (incidentally also of eclipse-dismissing) whenever the fancy took me.'

Grimble's experiences, by the way, formed the basis for the film *A Pattern of Islands*.

The beliefs of the people of Tibet, according to Lilith Babellon (representative in Wales of the Dalai Lama), are a blend of their original faith, called Bon, Indian Buddhism and Indian Tantra. Bon, she says, was ' ... an advanced form of animism perpetuated by shaman-priests called Bon Po. Magical practices played an integral role in living alongside the spirits of nature which animistic faiths perceive.' The Tibetans had – and apparently still have, in spite of Chinese Communist attempts to destroy their indigenous culture – a firm belief in the power of magic and spells.

They have their own form of psychic defence against malign influences – objects known as spirit traps. These ' ... are made from the skull of an animal, supported by a willow-rod framework interwoven with straw and woollen threads. When a form of negative energy is deemed caught, the entire trap is burned.'

In many parts of West Africa, black powder is used as a protection against malevolent witchcraft. It may be inserted in the bloodstream (like vaccination) through small cuts in the flesh, usually on the wrists, or mixed with water or palm wine and drunk. Children may be smeared twice a day with a cream containing the powder, and people too sick to be injected or to drink the powder-liquid may be painted with a mixture of the powder and palm oil. The powder is also often used medicinally, sprinkled or smeared on a sore; and some of the ingredients may, in fact, be herbal cures.

The recipe for the black powder varies from place to place. James H. Neal, in his book *Jungle Magic*, quotes one: 'The Ewe tribe make as a protection against witches a powder which is made of an aromatic mint called Amayi, plus certain parts of a squirrel, seven kinds of African incense, and also the African mistletoe. It is said that this powder is very protective, and Africans from many other far-away tribes go to the Ewe people to get their anti-witch protective powder.' (The use of the word 'witch' to translate the various local African words for 'malevolent spell-worker' has been an inevitable expression of European attitudes; and Neal – though a painstaking observer – was, after all, a colonial official.)

Charms and amulets are also worn as protection against 'witches' – usually necklaces or rings; the closer to the body they are, the more powerful they are considered to be.

Africans have their own forms of binding spell. Neal reports one, involving a padlock smeared with blood, which the fetish-priest held in his hand while he spoke the 'witch's' name several times and then 'locked her up with a key'. Apparently this compelled the culprit to come to him and confess.

Tuscany, in northern Italy, is one place where *la vecchia religione*, the Old Religion, has survived throughout Christian rule and, according to our contact, still flourishes. The lore and practices of Tuscan witchcraft were recorded at the end of the last century by Charles G. Leland in his book *Aradia: The Gospel of the Witches*.

This remarkable and many-talented American became a friend of a Tuscan witch called Maddalena and was initiated into her Craft himself. (He had a gift for being accepted by secretive peoples; he succeeded in the same way with Algonquin Indians and British Romanies.) Stewart describes Leland's character and achievements in his Introduction to the 1974 reprint of *Aradia* (see Bibliography).

Here are some of the Tuscan witch spells which Maddalena taught Leland.

A green lemon stuck full of pins of different colours always brings good fortune. Still better are a lemon, an orange and a mandarin, blessed with an invocation to Diana, beginning (in Leland's translation, which he gives after the Italian original):

> At the instant when the midnight came,
> I have picked a lemon in the garden,
> I have picked a lemon, and with it
> An orange and a (fragrant) mandarin.
> Gathering with care these (precious) things,
> And while gathering I said with care:
> 'Thou who art Queen of the sun and of the moon
> And of the stars – lo! here I call to thee!' ....

Leland points out that the orange represents the Sun, and the lemon the Moon – i.e., Diana herself.

A spell for a good grape crop involved going into the vineyard at the New Moon with a horn full of wine, drinking from the horn, kissing one's hand to the Moon and again invoking Diana:

> I drink, and yet it is not wine I drink,
> I drink the blood of Diana,
> Since from wine it has changed into her blood,
> And spread itself through all my growing vines....

(Kissing the hand to the New Moon is a very old practice. Job 31:26-8 condemns it as heathenish – and the basic material of Job is said to be the oldest in the Bible.)

A Tuscan love-spell, worked on a Friday, changes the desired woman ' ... into the form of a dog, when she, forgetting who she is, and all things besides, will at once come to his house, and there, when by him, take on her natural form again and remain with him. And when it is time for her to depart, she will again become a dog and go home, where she will turn into a girl. And she will remember nothing of what has taken place, or at least but little or mere fragments, which will seem as a confused dream. And she will take the form of a dog because Diana has ever a dog by her side.'

The invocation for this begins:

Diana, beautiful Diana!
Who art indeed as good as beautiful,
By all the worship I have given thee,
And all the joy of love which thou hast known,
I do implore thee aid me in my love!...


It is interesting that Diana, the supreme goddess of the Tuscan witches, is herself much older than the Roman state which adopted her.

Tuscan witches shared the universal belief in the magical value of a stone with a natural hole through it; they regarded it as a gift from Diana. Even an unholed but perfectly round stone was regarded as lucky – ' ... but it should never be given away, because the receiver will then get the good luck, and some disaster befall the giver'.

The Tuscan witch lore discovered by Leland has entered into the ritual of Gardnerian witchcraft. The opening of the Gardnerian Charge, from 'Whenever ye have need of anything' down to 'naked in your rites', is taken directly from *Aradia*.


Witchcraft among the Hopi Indians of America has a curious history. The Hopi (their name means 'Peace') have nine great religious ceremonies, but they once had ten, the tenth one being the Ya-Ya fire ceremony. It was based on contacting the spirits of the *tuvosi* (horned animal kingdom) for powerful magic, including imperviousness to burns, the lifting of 'impossible' weights, shape-changing into animal forms, and the ability to see in the dark or over long distances.

In one of the traditional Ya-Ya spells, the spell-worker would take a bowl of the white clay wash used for painting house walls, put his hands in it, make the motions of painting a wall and then point to a cliff miles away, which was suddenly painted white.

At first Ya-Ya magic was used entirely for the good of the people, but gradually some practitioners started using it for selfish ends. Then the people noticed that diseases of the eye were spreading among the Ya-Ya practitioners and decided that the system was evil. It was proscribed (reducing the great ceremonies once again to nine), first in one village and then in others, and its magical fetishes were sealed up in a cave where they still remain.

All this was centuries ago, but Ya-Ya survived in semi-secret right into the twentieth century in a corrupt form – which inevitably came to be known in English as 'witchcraft'.

The Ya-Ya story is told in detail in Frank Waters' fascinating *Book of the Hopi*.

The Hopis' spiritual philosophy is subtle and admirable; and they know perfectly well that workers of malign magic condemn themselves to their own destruction and to the loss of their powers.

Still in America, it seems that around the end of the eighteenth century and the beginning of the nineteenth, white Americans of all classes developed a passion for hunting buried treasure. (One of them was Joseph Smith, author – or transcriber from angelic dictation – of *The Book of Mormon.*) Pious Christians realized that such hunting smacked of magic, so they always dug with copies of the Bible, the Prayer Book and Bunyan's *Pilgrim's Progress* lying nearby, to fend off infernal spirits.

In 1786 Silas Hamilton, a prominent and wealthy (if rather oddly literate) citizen of Whittingham, Vermont, wrote in his notebook: 'A method to Tak up hid Treasure (viz.) Tak Nine Steel Rods about ten or twelve inches in Length Sharp or Piked to Perce in to the Erth, and let them be Besmeared with fresh blood from a hen mixed with hogdung. Then mak two Surkels a Little Larger in surcmuference than the hid Treasure lays in the Erth the other Surkel Sum Larger still, and as the hid treasure is wont to move to North or South East or west Place your Rods as is Discribed on the other side of this leaf' – with an accompanying sketch, now in the Lee Library at the Brigham Young University.

This spell (it can be called nothing else) would appear useless at first sight, since it could be used only when the site of the treasure was already pinpointed, but in fact it was a form of binding spell, to prevent demons from moving the treasure – though there would appear to be two opinions as to whether the mover was a demon or an angel. That other Mormon pioneer Brigham Young (also a native of Whittingham), declared decades later: 'These treasures that are in the earth are carefully watched, they can be moved from place to place according to the good pleasure of Him who made them and owns them. He has his messengers at his service, and it is just as easy for an angel to remove the minerals from any part of these mountains to another, as it is for you and me to walk up and down this hall.'

We can only hope that Silas Hamilton did not inadvertently offend any treasure-moving angels.

# XIV  *Spells of the People*

English shepherds once counted their sheep (and in some places perhaps still do) in a way they believed to bring luck. Instead of the usual 'one, two, three ...' they would count:

Yan, Tan, Tethera, Pethera, Pimp,
Sethera, Lethera, Hovera, Dovera, Dik,
Yan-a-Dik, Tan-a-Dik, Tethera-Dik

– and so on. Doreen Valiente (*Where Witchcraft Lives*, p. 72) reports this custom from Sussex, while Stewart heard of it in East Anglia and Janet in Leyton on the edge of Epping Forest. It clearly stems from P-Celtic, the family to which Welsh, Cornish and Breton belong (four and five in Welsh, for example, are *pedwar* and *pump*, in Cornish *paswar* and *pymp*, and in Breton *peder* and *pemp*). It may well, as Doreen suggests, come from a form of British Celtic older than the Anglo-Saxon conquest. But the 'Tethera, Pethera, Sethera, Lethera' and 'Hovera, Dovera' pattern-repetitions, which depart entirely from

105

the three languages mentioned, suggest to us that, over the centuries since Celtic counting ceased to correspond to everyday speech, it has been distorted by the instinct to make magical words into a rhythmic and memorable jingle.

Cornish fishermen, incidentally, were still counting their catch in Cornish long after the language had ceased to be used in everyday speech.

Janet's grandfather, who was a devout Christian, knew of the shepherds' count and regarded it as suspect and possibly devilish – a common enough reaction to puzzling items of folklore. Yet, oddly enough, it was his habit to beat his apple trees with a stick on Twelfth Night – 'to make the sap rise', he explained to Janet. He cannot have realized that this was straight sympathetic magic, the traditional English custom of 'wassailing' or 'worsling' (from the Old Norse *'ves heill'*, 'be in health'). Wassailing involved ritual stick-beating of the whole apple orchard during the Twelve Days of Christmas, to the chanting of a fertility song. Doreen Valiente (*ibid.*, p. 62) gives a Sussex version of the song:

> Stand fast, root,
> Bear well, top,
> Pray the God send us
> A good bowling crop.
> Every twig, apples big,
> Every bough, apples enow.
> Hats full, caps full,
> Full quarters, sacks full!

*Where Witchcraft Lives* is, incidentally, a rich mine of the magical lore of Doreen's home county of Sussex, and well worth reading by students of spell-working. One more example of it (from p. 73) before we leave it. Sussex women who were anxious to have a baby used the sympathetic magic of rocking an empty cradle. The traditional rhyme promised them:

> If you rock the cradle empty,
> Then you shall have babies plenty.

One spell which every child knows (and many adults half-humorously continue to use) is to say 'Hares' just before midnight on the last day of the month, and 'Rabbits, rabbits, hares and rabbits' (or a local variant thereof) on the first day of the new month, before you or anyone in your hearing says anything else. This is supposed to ensure good luck for the whole of the month.

There is, of course, the other children's one – 'A pinch and a punch, first day of the month, and no returns', with the corresponding action. We wonder if this, too, was once a good-luck spell, which has degenerated into mere oneupmanship?

When two people say the same thing at the same time, the quickest thinker pinches the other, with the words 'A pinch for you and a surprise for me.'

When you see the first star of the evening (which will probably be the planet Venus), you recite:

Star light, star bright,
First star I've seen tonight,
I wish I may, I wish I might,
Have the wish I wish tonight

– and wish. You then wait to see a second star, or your wish will not come true.

Ginny, our coven Maiden, admits she is cautious about this one: if the night is at all cloudy, she will wish only a small wish – so that if the second star fails to appear, she won't have lost anything important!

Irish witchcraft and spell-working have a character of their own. There is little evidence of consciously non-Christian covens in Irish history; these did not materialize until the twentieth-century Craft revival in Britain reached Ireland in the 1970s, and if any existed before, they kept themselves successfully secret. While the rest of Europe was going mad and executing witches (whether actual or supposed) in their millions, Ireland's witch trials, between the first in 1324 and the last in 1711, could be counted on two hands.

The Irish pattern took (and in places still takes) two basic forms. One is the village *bean feasa* (wisewoman) or *fear feasa* (wiseman), pronounced 'ban fassa' and 'far fassa'. The other is the survival of transparently pagan folk customs. Both operate within a nominally Christian framework, the Church's attitude ranging from worried disapproval (as with many a *bean feasa*) to the attachment of a saint's name to a custom and claiming that it is really Christian (as with Midsummer – 'St John's Eve' – bonfires and the springtime rituals of Bridget's Crosses).

The first and most renowned of the Irish witch trials was that of Dame Alice Kyteler (pronounced 'Kittler') of Kilkenny in 1324. It was instigated by Richard de Ledrede, Bishop of Ossory, described by the seneschal of Kilkenny as a 'vile, rustic, interloping monk'. French-trained, the bishop seems to have had ambitions to introduce into Ireland the fanatical concepts and methods of the Continental persecution. His charges were all the standard ones, including denial of God, traffic with demons, nocturnal sabbats, spells to kill or injure men and livestock, and sexual intercourse with a mysterious man in black called Robin Artisson, who had a rod of iron and could shape-change and to whom sacrifices were made.

Dame Alice was able to call on influential help and even managed to imprison the bishop for a while after he had excommunicated her. Finally she escaped to England, and the bishop tried her lady's maid, Petronilla de Meath, as a scapegoat, flogging her repeatedly till she 'confessed' to all the charges, and then burned her alive.

No other Irish witch trial quite reached this level of drama and brutality.

Alice Kyteler's substantial house still stands in Kilkenny; it is now a hotel, with a restaurant in the cellar where it is said her coven used to meet.

Still to be seen, too, is the humble cottage of the most famous *bean feasa* of them all, Biddy Early, who lived in Co. Clare in the last century and whom W.B. Yeats in one of his poems called 'wise Biddy Early'. She was famous both for her cures and for her clairvoyance; time and again she would tell people why they had come before they told her, and describe scenes and events which she had no 'normal' way of knowing about. She was generous and hospitable, treating rich and poor alike, but uncompromising in her advice.

Biddy possessed a bottle which she used as others use a crystal ball or tea-leaves, and there are many stories about that bottle. Some say that when her son helped the fairies to win a hurling match, they gave it to him for his mother. When she died, some say the bottle was thrown into a nearby lough (some people have actually dragged for it), while others maintain it had to be broken before the priest would give her a Christian burial.

Lady Gregory was able to interview a number of local people who had known her, and she gives twenty pages of their fascinating accounts in her book *Visions and Beliefs in the West of Ireland* (see Bibliography).

One old man told her: 'The priests were greatly against Biddy Early. And there's no doubt that it was from the faeries that she got the knowledge. But who wouldn't go to hell for a cure if one of his own was sick? And the priests don't like to be doing cures themselves. Father Flynn said to me, if I do them, I let the devil into me.' (This belief crops up repeatedly, that priests can cure but are extremely reluctant to do so – ' ... unless they're curates that like to get the money,' one source adds.)

Apparently she disarmed one priest at least. Mary Glyn told Lady Gregory: 'It is Biddy Early had the great name, but the priests were against her. There went a priest one time to stop her, and when he came near the door the horse fell that was in his car. Biddy Early came out then and bid him to give three spits on the horse, and he did that, and it rose up then and there. It was himself had put the evil eye on it. "It was yourself did it, you bodach," she said to the priest. And he said, "You may do what you like from this out, and I will not meddle with you again." '

We cannot resist quoting one more eye-witness, a Mrs Locke: 'Mrs Brennan, in the house beyond, went one time to Biddy Early, where the old man was losing his health. All she told him was to bid him give over drinking so much whiskey. So after she said that, he used only to be drinking gin.'

One thing Alice Kyteler and Biddy Early had in common: both outlived several husbands. In Dame Alice's case, as one might expect, her detractors put a sinister interpretation on this, but no one seems to have done the same with Biddy Early. Her husbands, apparently, all drank themselves to death. 'Wild cards they were,' one Daniel Curtin told Lady Gregory, 'or they wouldn't have married her.'

An interesting example of pagan spell-working comes from a middle-aged Dublin friend of ours. When he was a child in Co. Longford, his good Catholic parents would take the whole family out into the young crops to dance naked at midnight on May Eve. They were told that this would protect them against colds for the coming year – but the ritual was clearly a crop-fertility spell, with the health-protecting excuse instilled into the children in case word got out.

An Irish cure for 'the rose', known medically as erysipelas and in Gaelic as *ruiadhe*, included both physical treatment and a spell. One applied a poultice of scalded flour to stop the sore from spreading, and on the outside of the poultice one wrote the first name and surname of the patient. The writing must be done by someone of the same surname as the patient or, even better, of the same first name as well. (Erysipelas seems to have been regarded as particularly susceptible to magic, both to cure and to cause. A Scottish Highland spell involved cutting a lock of hair – preferably red – into snippets and throwing it, with curses, at the intended victim; a sore would develop for each snippet.)

An Irish spell to cure mumps was to wear a donkey's blinkers or bridle while drinking at a well or river. If the patient was a child, his or her head was rubbed against the back of a pig with the words '*Muc, Muc, seo dhuit do leici*' ('Pig, Pig, here are your mumps'). The disease would then be transferred to the pig.

A donkey also entered into the traditional cure for a child's whooping-cough. The child was passed three times over and round the animal's back and belly.

A cure for headache was to put leaves of the wood anemone (*bainne-bo-bliatain*) on your head.

We cannot answer for the effectiveness of these cures; but it was in the West of Ireland (where folk customs tend to survive more strongly than elsewhere) that we discovered that the expression 'hair of the dog that bit you' has a literal meaning. A woman in our village was bitten by a neighbour's dog – more or less accidentally, since the dog knew her and was not hostile – and the bite-mark became septic. So she went to the dog, spoke to him friendlily and took a hair from his coat. This hair she bound over the wound. Within days it had healed, without a mark left. Whether this result was magical or psychosomatic or came from some unrealized chemical reaction, we must admit we don't know; but the treatment certainly worked.

Bullawn stones (rocks with cup-shaped depressions on top which gather water) were and still are regarded as magically powerful; the water from them is used to cure everything from warts to barrenness. Many of these stones are, in fact, probably grain-milling stones dating from megalithic times.

One curious Irish tradition is that for each man or woman there is one hour in the day in which he or she will be able to have a wish granted, and also be able to see spirits; but what hour this is can be discovered only by trial and error.

It was considered unlucky to be on the third boat to leave harbour; so, as a protective measure, sometimes the first three boats would lash themselves together, so that, with a literally tied first, there was strictly speaking no third.

A newly married bride was believed to have the power to calm a storm at sea. (We came across this belief ourselves on the Co. Mayo coast.) Whitsuntide sailings were said to invite drowning, and some people would not sail then unless a bride was at the helm. (A child born at Whitsun used to be laid briefly in a newly dug grave to ward off the Whitsun dangers from it.)

A bride was also held to have power over the fairies – provided she did not lift both feet off the floor at the same time in a dance; if she did, they gained power over her.

If a farmer's milk would not churn into butter, he would suspect a neighbour's curse. (See also p. 122 below.) The counter-spell was to wrap the chains from his plough round the churn.

A hazel rod was a good protective charm to carry with you, turning it around now and then; if you did, it was said, 'No bad thing can hurt you.'

St Martin's Day, 11 November, used to be a day when special protection of the house was called for, by spilling the blood of newly killed cocks at the house corners (sometimes even in the corners of all the rooms) and stuffing rags soaked in their blood in the rafters. It was considered unlucky to go on a journey on St Martin's Eve or St Martin's Day. As in many old customs, this date may reflect a conservative clinging to the old Julian calendar – in which case, this particular tradition was originally a Hallowe'en (Samhain) one.

Irish girls used to hunt for a snail in the grass on May morning for a divination spell. Placed on a plate of flour, the snail would move around, writing the initials of the boy the girl would marry. Another way was to eat an apple in front of her mirror at midnight on Hallowe'en, when she would see her future husband in the glass.

There seem to have been different husband-identifying spells for different times of the year. That for the first full Moon of the new year was rather complicated. The girl would take a black-handled knife (interesting!) and cut three pieces of earth with it. These she had to take home, tie them in her left stocking and secure it with her right garter. This bundle she put under her pillow at night. She also had to gather certain herbs, while she recited:

> Moon, Moon, tell unto me
> When my true love I shall see?
> What fine clothes am I to wear?
> How many children will I bear?
> For if my love comes not to me,
> Dark and dismal my life will be

– doubtless an English rendering of a Gaelic original. She would then, in her sleep, dream of her future husband.

A round-the-year method was for the girl to throw a ball of wool into a lime-kiln, keeping the loose end in her hand and winding it up till an invisible hand seemed to hold it tight. She would then ask who held the wool, and a voice would tell her who her future husband would be.

The Scottish habit of first-footing, arranging for a dark-haired man to be the first to enter the house in the first minutes of Hogmanay, New Year's Day, to ensure good luck for the coming year, appears in Ireland too – but attached to the first Monday in January, known as Handsel Monday ('handsel' being an old word for a New Year good-luck gift).

It is interesting how, in this Catholic country, even malignant spells may be expressed in Christian terms. For example, to break up a pair of lovers, one throws a handful of clay from a new grave between them, saying: 'Hate ye one another! May ye be as hateful to each other as sin is to Christ, or as bread eaten without blessing is to God!' And is not stealing clay from a grave a form of sacrilege?

The gypsies have a simple, two-word money spell of their own. It is to repeat the phrase 'Trinka five' to yourself several times whenever you need cash. We must admit we've found it often works – though we still don't know what 'Trinka' means, and neither of the Romany-blood friends we've asked has been able to tell us. Or do they fear the spell may lose its power if they give away the secret?

Romany tradition divides magic into black and white. On the one hand, the malevolent spells of the *cohani*; on the other, the helpful magic of the *drabarni*. *Drabarni* (from *drab*, grass or herb) means 'herb-woman', for much of her supposed magic is, in fact, straightforward herbal medicine. But animals also play a big part in Romany magical lore.

Among the Kalderash, an important group of European metalworking gypsies, 15 March is the Feast of the Serpent. Anyone who manages to kill a snake on that day will have good fortune all year. Sea-urchin fossils are called snakes' eyes and used as good-luck amulets. On the malignant side, the *cohani* use powdered snakeskin in malevolent philtres.

Weasels, on the other hand, are dreaded but must not be killed, or the whole tribe will have bad luck. The weasel puffs when it is afraid or angry, and gypsies call it 'the blower'; its puff is identified with the Devil's sneezing. If a caravan meets a weasel, especially if it puffs, the caravan must change course. If an engaged girl is puffed at by a weasel, she must wash herself in a running stream, or her marriage will be unhappy.

(The Irish, too, used to believe that to meet a weasel was unlucky – it might be a shape-changed spiteful witch; but to kill one was even worse. If you did, you must immediately kill one of your own hens and hang it from a post in the farmyard, to counter the bad luck. Incidentally, what the English call a weasel, the Irish call a stoat; the English stoat is not found in Ireland.)

The squirrel (Romany *morga*, 'gypsy cat') brings good luck, especially in love. Best luck-bringer of all, though, is the hedgehog (*niglo*).

The malevolent magic of the *cohani* makes use of the pricking of wax images; but other forms of attack are less well known outside Romany lore – for example, gathering grass at a crossroads and placing it under the entrance to the intended victim's tent or caravan; or watering a branch of weeping willow for nine days and then pouring that water in front of the same entrance.

Protective spells against such malice, and against the Evil Eye (*iachalipe*), are particularly carefully practised where children may be threatened. One way is to pour a child's bathwater over him or her, so that it runs along the blade of a scythe on the way down – evil spirits hating contact with iron. Another was to tie a violin string, or a piece of red string, round the child's wrist; yet another, to lick his or her eye three times, spitting between licks.

Gypsies have a spell for a pregnant woman who wants to know if she is carrying a boy or girl. She should go into a garden where red and white roses are growing close together, and spin around in front of the bushes eleven times with her eyes shut, moving from East to West (which presumably means starting facing East and spinning deosil, if she wants to stay close to the bushes). She should then reach out, with her eyes still shut, and pick a rose. If it is white, her child will be a girl; if it is red, a boy.

Leaving gypsies for the more general folk-spells of Britain – another spell involving roses is for a woman to bring a desired lover to her. She should walk naked through the garden by moonlight, scattering rose petals behind her while she holds the image of the man in her mind.

To bring a wayward lover to heel also involved roses. The girl gathered three on Midsummer Eve, buried one under a yew tree soon after midnight, put the second in a newly dug grave and put the third under her pillow, where she left it for three nights before taking it out and burning it. Her lover would then know no peace till he returned to her.

A girl could also use a rose picked on Midsummer Eve for a husband-identifying spell. She would wrap it in white paper and put it away till Christmas Day. If it was still fresh, she would wear it to church, and her destined husband would come and take it. If it had faded, the omens were bad.

In Yorkshire, a girl about to be married could ensure the number of sons and daughters she wanted by making a straw garter. She would go to the hayricks secretly on a Friday night and collect a wheat straw for every boy child she wanted, and an oat straw for every girl. She would plait these into a garter and wear it round her leg from Friday evening to Monday morning. If it stayed in place, the spell would work. There were two provisos: her husband-to-be must know nothing of the spell, or it would fail; and she must be a virgin at the time, or harm would come to all her children.

To find out if your lover will marry you, one folk-custom is to float two acorns in a bowl of water, naming each of them for one of you. If they float close together, marriage is predicted; but if they float away from each other, there is no future in the relationship.

At Hallowe'en, the same question was asked of two hazel nuts, which were put on the bars of the grate. If they moved towards each other, the relationship would blossom, but if they moved apart, the questioner's lover was unfaithful.

Nuts of all kinds, particularly hazel and the phallic-looking acorn, are frequent symbols in fertility or love spells. An acorn carried in the pocket is a charm to keep yourself young.

In Devonshire, it was the custom at weddings for an old woman to present the bride with a bag of hazel nuts as she came out of the church, to ensure the fruitfulness of her marriage. At Gaillac in France, bride and groom were pelted with nuts while they were still at the altar, and in Poitou the floor of the wedding-breakfast room was strewn with nuts. In Ancient Rome, nuts were given to newly married couples. All these customs had the same significance – as had doubtless, at one time, the modern custom of confetti-throwing.

Oranges have the same fertility symbolism, particularly at weddings, in the countries where they grow; and when orangeries became a feature of well-to-do country houses in England, their symbolism was imported, and orange blossom became a traditional bridal flower.

One wedding-spell which everybody knows, and most brides still observe even if only as a pleasant bit of tradition, is that the bride's outfit should include 'something old, something new, something borrowed and something blue'.

It is still considered good magic for the bride to delay being completely dressed and veiled until she is ready to leave for the wedding. This is sometimes achieved by fitting the dress in sections, one at a time, or by leaving one hem unstitched until the last moment. In particular, the bride must not see herself fully arrayed (especially with her veil in place) in a mirror before that last moment. And above all, of course, the groom must not see her on the wedding morning until she walks up the aisle.

In a sense, all this reflects the concept of rebirth which is central to all rites of passage; the bride is starting a new life, and the ritual of her dressing, emergence and unveiling before the altar for her man's kiss, dramatize the fact appropriately – as does the favourite colour for wedding dresses, white. In Shropshire, the bride used to emphasize this concept in private as well, by stripping completely naked before she started to array herself, and nothing she put on had ever been worn or used by her before.

This 'new life' concept may also underlie the tradition of the groom carrying the bride over the doorstep of her new home. She does not walk from one life to another; she starts her new life from scratch, so to speak, with her feet on its ground 'out of thin air'. Though another interpretation is possible – that it enshrines the abduction ritual which still survives in some countries, whereby the groom pretends to kidnap his bride from her parental home, and her relatives pretend to try to recapture her. Where this does survive, it is little more than a cheerful romp; but it may at one time have been serious ... Like many folk customs, carrying the bride over the threshold may stem from more than one original concept.

The veil is regarded as particularly magical. A veil which is a family heirloom, or borrowed from a friend whose marriage has proved happy, endows the wedding with the good fortune of the earlier wearers.

The wedding cake has always been, and still is, one of the central spell-working features of the marriage ritual. Its rich ingredients are to ensure the good things of life for the couple. The bride has to cut the cake, to ensure her own fecundity – and the symbolism of the husband's hand laid over hers as she does so, and the use of his sword if he has one, is unambiguous. Every guest has to have a piece, so that all support the magic – and pieces are sent to absent friends for the same purpose. An unmarried girl who puts her piece under her pillow at night will dream of her future husband.

These wedding-cake customs are still pretty well universal; but there are others which used to be observed, and perhaps in some places still are. For example, the would-be dreamer used to pass a crumb of her piece of cake three or nine times through a wedding ring before putting it under her pillow. And the bride used to keep a piece carefully to ensure her husband's faithfulness. Sometimes she would keep a piece until the first child was born, to be eaten at its christening feast.

The cake-plate itself used to be thrown over the bride's head and broken, and the pattern of the pieces studied for divination – sometimes to indicate the number of children.

Witches have their own addition to the wedding-cake spell: that this is the only occasion when the athame or ritual sword may be used for actual cutting.

We saw above that Irish girls had particular dates for working spells to identify their future husbands. English girls worked such spells particularly on Hallowe'en, Christmas Eve, St Agnes's Eve (20 January) and St Mark's Eve (24 April). The spells frequently involved Dumb Cakes, made of flour, water, eggs and salt. They could be made alone or by two or more girls together. The only common factor was that the whole thing must be done without uttering a word – hence the name Dumb Cake.

The Sun-like little flower St John's wort, which blooms around Midsummer, could be picked by a woman who wanted to be pregnant, walking naked in the garden. She would give birth before next Midsummer. If a girl gathered it in the morning dew of St John's Eve, 23 June, before she had eaten anything, she would marry within the year; sleeping with it under her pillow that night would show her her future husband in a dream.

St John's wort used to be called *Fuga daemonum* because it drove away evil spirits and protected houses against haunting and malignant spells.

> Trefoil, vervain, John's wort, dill,
> Hinder witches of their will.

One husband-identifying spell allowed the girl to short-list the possible men. She would scratch the name of each man on an onion and put all the onions in a warm place. The first onion to sprout would identify the destined husband.

Ivy leaves were used in many places for this form of divination. In Oxfordshire, the girl would put a leaf in her pocket, and the first man she met would be her husband-to-be – even if he were married already. In northern Scotland, she put it against her heart, saying:

> Ivy, Ivy, I love you,
> In my bosom I put you.
> The first young man who speaks to me
> My future husband he shall be.

Cardiganshire people used ivy leaves for a variant of the hazels-on-the-grate spell we mentioned above. Two ivy leaves were put on the fire at Hallowe'en; if they moved together as they burned, so would the lovers; if they moved apart or failed to burn, the lovers would quarrel and break up.

The dew of May Day morning has always had many magical uses. Gathered very early, if possible from under an oak tree, it would make a woman who bathed her face in it beautiful for the whole year. This particular spell need not be worked in private: the May-morning dew-washing used to be a women's social occasion. *Pepy's Diary* mentions Mrs Pepys joining in such a feminine get-together on 1 May 1667.

Morning dew in general, but May Day dew most powerfully of all, was gathered or walked in as a cure for goitre, sore eyes and skin troubles, and sniffed up the nose for vertigo.

In the Balkans, May morning dew was rubbed on cattle to protect them against malevolent witchcraft for the coming year.

A nineteenth-century work tells how two Scottish witches brushed dew from the grass on May morning with a hair-tether. The tether was then hung in a cow-byre, and the cows produced so much milk that there were not enough containers to hold it.

Kipling sums up the original spell-working purpose of May Eve/May Day rituals in his *Tree Song*:

> Oh, do not tell the Priest our plight,
>   Or he would call it sin;
> But – we have been out in the woods all night,
>   A-conjuring Summer in!

– which verse, with 'plight' amended to 'art', has become part of the Gardnerian Beltane ritual.

When the Iron Age began to transform the known world, from about the sixth century BC onwards, its impact upon those peoples who were still using bronze was traumatic. Bronze weapons were effective mainly by the blows they could inflict; iron weapons actually cut. Naturally, iron acquired a magical reputation, particularly among aboriginal peoples overrun by iron-using invaders.

This concept, that iron possesses magical power, persisted long after the metal was in virtually universal use, and traces of it are still to be found today. Blacksmiths and farriers, who possessed and had mastery of its secrets, were regarded as natural magicians, to be treated with wary respect. Iron Age craftsmanship deities – Hephaestus, Vulcan, Wayland the Smith and the rest – were all primarily blacksmiths, whatever other secondary skills, such as jewellery-making, they might possess.

This attitude survives, for example, in one folk-custom that is still universal. Horseshoes as good-luck symbols are displayed points upwards, so that the luck shall not run out – except by blacksmiths, who still nail them on their forge doors points-downwards, the original purpose having been to pour their magical power onto the forge itself. One wonders how many of today's blacksmiths still believe, if only subconsciously, in that 'original' purpose.

Some blacksmiths do seem to have retained a conscious sense of their magical status. As one of them told Lady Gregory, when talking about the cures of *bean feasa* Biddy Early (see p. 108 above): 'I never went to her myself – for you should know that no ill or harm ever comes to a blacksmith.'

Water from the trough in a forge, if you could manage to steal it, was said to cure all ailments.

Valerie Worth (*The Crone's Book of Words*, p. 77) give a horseshoe spell to cure a headache. You hold one end in each hand, press the centre against your forehead, and recite:

Good metal loosed
From horse's hoof,
Draw from my brain
These nails of pain;
Cast them away,
Rust them away,
Keep them away.

There is a belief among taxi-drivers that it is lucky to have a letter U (or, even better, two Us) in the cab's registration number, because of its horseshoe shape. (They also like to have a 7, or multiples of 7, in the number.)

Iron nails driven into cradles or the beds of women in childbirth, or a pair of scissors left under cushions or carpets, were placed there as a protective spell. The protective driving of iron nails into house walls is as old as Ancient Rome, where it was said to be particularly effective against the plague.

In Suffolk, one cured the ague by going to a crossroads, turning round three times, driving a tenpenny nail into the ground while the clock was striking midnight, and walking away backwards before the last note of the bell had died away. Rather a selfish spell, this one, because the next person to walk over the nail would contract the disease you had got rid of.

Less anti-social was the nail cure for toothache. You scratched the gum with a new nail till it bled, and then hammered the nail into an oak tree, the toothache going with it.

Talking of crossroads – suicides or executed witches buried there would often have an iron spike driven through the corpse to prevent the spirit rising to haunt the living.

It was believed that a suspected witch could be tested by secretly driving a nail into her footprint. If she was indeed a witch, she would feel a burning in her foot and be compelled to go to the place and draw the nail out of the footprint. If she was not, she would be unaffected by it.

Needles and pins naturally shared a lot of the reputation of nails and would be stuck in doorposts for protective purposes. They were also, as we have seen, used malignantly in image-pricking.

An interesting counter-spell to suspected image-pricking comes from Sussex. A jar full of pins was put by the fire; as the pins became hot, so the attacker would suffer and be compelled to desist.

To find and pick up a dropped nail or pin, provided it is not pointing towards you, is still considered fortunate:

See a pin and pick it up,
All the day you'll have good luck.

In the days when bridesmaids used to take the bride to the marital bedroom and undress her, there was a race to get the first pin, because the bridesmaid who succeeded would be the first to marry. (Very similar to the race to catch the bride's thrown bouquet today.) But all the pins must be carefully gathered, taken out of the bedroom and thrown away. If one were left in the bedroom, it would bring bad luck to the bride; and if a bridesmaid kept one, she would not marry before Whitsuntide.

Knives in particular have always been credited with iron-magic. A knife stuck into the woodwork of a cradle, or into the door of a house, served the same protective function we have mentioned. One might also be stuck into the mast of a fishing-boat for the same reason – though sailors regarded it as unlucky to use the word 'knife' at sea.

A knife with a white handle was used to discover whether your future husband or wife would be dark or fair. You had to spin it on the table; if it came to rest pointing towards you, your partner would be dark, or if away from you, fair.

For witches, the athame or black-handled knife is the most important magical tool of all, because it is personal, while most of the others are joint coven property. It is not touched by anyone else without asking permission first. A witch will consciously work to charge the athame with his or her personal essence. Circles are cast either with the athame or with its coven-property equivalent, the sword. Athame and sword must never be used for actual cutting – with the traditional exception of a wedding or hand-fasting cake, as we mentioned earlier.

For any actual cutting or inscribing which has to be done in the Circle, the white-handled knife must be used; this tool is coven property.

The black-handled and white-handled knives are used in the same way by ritual magicians; they are described in *The Key of Solomon*.

In the days when long-distance communication was almost non-existent, and most people could not write, a knife was used in one of several spells to know how an absent person was faring. His knife would be kept, and as long as the blade remained bright, all was well; if it became dull, he was in trouble; and if it rusted badly or broke, he was dead, and the family would go into mourning. The clothes he had left behind were watched for deterioration in the same way.

Presumably families would work positive magic by seeing to it that such rusting or deterioration did not occur.

Another form of this spell was to keep a sample of the absent one's urine in a securely corked bottle. If it remained clear or became cloudy or dried up, the same three conclusions were drawn. The only positive magic possible in this case would be to see that the bottle was spotlessly clean to start with!

One spell we must all have used at one time or another without even realizing that it was a spell – namely, spitting on our hands (or at least miming the action) before undertaking some physical action, whether work or a fight. This used to be done to enhance one's strength and to increase the chances of success or victory. Spittle, like blood, used to be regarded as a carrier of one's life-essence, and therefore as a source of power.

It used to be customary to spit on a friend who was starting on a journey or about to undertake some difficult task, to ensure his or her good luck. Spitting also emphasized the truth of a statement or the sincerity of a promise:

> Finger wet, finger dry,
> Cut my throat if I tell a lie.

Spittle was used, too, as a cure for warts, ringworm and other skin troubles.

A Cornish spell to kill an adder was to draw a circle round it on the ground (at a safe distance, presumably), mark a cross inside the circle and recite the first two verses of the 68th Psalm: 'Let God arise, let his enemies be scattered; let them also that hate him flee before him. As smoke is driven away, so drive them away; as wax melteth before the fire, so let the wicked perish at the presence of God' – which seems to us rather a harsh categorization of a creature which strikes only when it feels itself threatened. However, once dead, the adder was regarded as having beneficial uses. In Lincolnshire, adder's flesh was boiled with a chicken to make 'hetherd-broth', taken to treat consumption, while in other places a dried adder's skin was hung in the roof to bring good luck and protect the house against fire.

Perhaps because Ireland has no snakes, and St Patrick is popularly supposed to have banished them from the island, Irishmen were believed also to have power over them. A North of England tradition said that, if an Irishman drew a circle round an adder or a toad, the animal would be trapped in it and die. If a dog was bitten by an adder, the wound could be healed by washing it with milk from an Irish cow. Even stones from Ireland could be used to protect a house from snakes, toads and frogs; and this belief about Irish stones, and samples of earth, seems to have been widespread in northern Europe.

Not only Europe. Our coven Maiden, Ginny Russell, was born in Australia, and she tells us of one well-to-do Australian whose home was troubled by snakes. He had a load of earth imported from Ireland, which was put in a trench completely encircling the house. No snake crossed the trench thereafter.

(It has been suggested that there is some factor – maybe a microscopic fungus – in Irish soil to which snakes are allergic; but apparently the question is still unsettled.)

One very persistent folk-belief is that what a pregnant woman thinks about will affect the character and abilities of the child, and many women shape their thinking deliberately to this end. Stewart's mother, for example, read all the good literature she could lay her hands on while she was carrying him; and it must be admitted that he has never wanted to be anything but a writer from the time he could read (which was before he went to school).

If a woman finds many little things going wrong in her housework, tradition says she can change her luck by turning her apron back-to-front; and putting it on back-to-front in the first place is considered lucky, provided it is done accidentally and left there.

She could not sweep dust outwards from the house, because dust is identified with the home's prosperity (and not only in the British Isles). To conserve that prosperity, she should sweep the dust inwards. Having collected it all together, she may then safely gather it into a dustpan or whatever and carry it outside.

One of the charges against Dame Alice Kyteler (see p. 107 above) was that she robbed her neighbours by sweeping their dust from their front doors to her own, saying:

> To the house of William my son
> Hie all the wealth of Kilkenny town.

Another tip for housewives: tea-leaves are used not only for divination. A Worcestershire belief is that to scatter them on the ground in front of the house is a protection against evil spirits.

A card-player, it is said, can end a run of bad luck by standing up and turning round three times with his chair. On the other hand, one can end an opponent's good luck by waiting till he throws a used match into the ashtray, and surreptitiously placing another crosswise over it. (Simple counter-spell: either don't smoke when you are playing cards, or use a lighter!)

Stewart and one of our witches, Marjorie, were in her local pub one day, and four men were playing poker. Marjorie whispered: 'That poor man is always losing. Let's give him a hand.' So, standing unobtrusively behind him, they willed cool thinking and good luck towards him. He won four very profitable hands in a row.

'Perhaps we should feel guilty about that,' Marjorie said after they'd left. 'But he's a nice sucker who deserves a break, so I don't.'

Neither did Stewart.

Rainwater is believed in many places to have magical powers. Rain falling on Ascension Day used to be collected and kept as a cure for many ailments, especially for weak or sore eyes. In Wales, babies bathed in rainwater were believed to speak earlier than others, and money washed in rainwater could not be stolen.

Traditions about good-luck actions sometimes contradict each other. Some believe a bed should be placed along a North–South line (a belief incidentally shared by that pioneer of sex education Dr Marie Stopes) and that an East–West alignment will bring restlessness and nightmares, while others hold exactly the opposite view. At least the North–South school gives a reason, whether scientifically meaningful or not: that the North–South placing harmonizes with the natural magnetic currents of the Earth.

Again, in some places it is considered lucky, and in others highly unlucky, to plant a potato crop on Good Friday.

Another flat contradiction is between the British belief that a black cat is lucky, and the American one that it is unlucky. But then the cat throughout history seems to have symbolized either extreme good or extreme evil; it has never been neutral.

To look at bad-luck actions for a moment (refraining from which can be called a kind of good-luck spell), there is one English tradition which still seems to be observed: that it is extremely unlucky to kill a robin or to damage its nest or eggs. The reason for this may be forgotten but seems plain: the robin is the bird of the God of the Waxing Year, so to harm him is to offend against the return of life and fertility to the Earth. The wren, on the other hand, is the bird of the God of the Waning Year, and the ritual of hunting and killing him at midwinter is still observed in many folk customs, fortunately only symbolically. It is significant that the robin is a favourite feature of Christmas cards, which after all celebrate the turning of the year from waning to waxing.

Another practice to refrain from: the popular saying about someone having 'got out of bed on the wrong side' has its root in the old belief that, to ensure good luck, one should always get out of bed on the same side as one got into it.

Dried frogs, toads, black beetles and spiders have all been hung round the neck in little silk bags as healing spells; and the unfortunate frog has sometimes been stuck with pins and otherwise tormented, like a living wax image, to bring pain to an enemy or an unfaithful lover.

A piece of sulphur carried round, or taken to bed, with you is said to prevent or cure rheumatism and cramp.

The hand-churning of butter was always a tricky business, so a south Midlands spell for its success involved repeating this rhyme as you churned:

Come, butter, churn,

Come, butter, come.
The great Bull of Banbury
Shan't have none.

Other districts had their own rhymes for the same purpose.

If the churn or its handle was made of rowan wood, this would protect it against malignant witchcraft, to which the process of churning was believed to be very vulnerable.

The rowan, or mountain ash, has always been regarded as a magical tree. It is said to be found particularly round megalithic stone circles and known druidic holy places, suggesting that its magical reputation is very ancient indeed. In Finland, it was the sacred tree of the Earth-Mother goddess Rauni, as her name emphasizes. In some places in Britain it is known as the wicken-tree or witch-tree. All too often, since the persecution centuries, the word 'witch' has been used only to mean malignant spell-workers, as in the Scottish rhyme:

Rowan tree and red threid
Gar the witches tyne their speed

– and rowan branches or berries were used in a host of different ways for the magical protection of homes and people. In some districts, the day for placing these was Rowan Day, 3 May. In Yorkshire,

If your whipstock's made of rowan
You may ride your nag through any town.

Witches were reputed to be able to draw milk from a cow at a distance – and one protection against this was a twig of rowan stuck through the cow's tail hair.

A rowan twig was part of a collection of items, obviously intended as magical charms, found in a Bronze Age grave in Denmark.

The rowan was frequently planted in Scottish graveyards to keep out evil magic. A famous example is the grave at Manor Churchyard, Peeblesshire, of David Ritchie, whom Sir Walter Scott made the prototype of his novel *The Black Dwarf*. Ritchie was afraid of witchcraft, and it was his dying wish to have his grave surrounded by rowan trees – which can still be seen.

Children born with a caul (a thin membrane over their heads) were considered extremely lucky. Cauls were always kept as protective charms, especially by sailors for protection against drowning. As late as 1944, a woman in Oxfordshire was offered £10 (a considerable sum in those days) for her baby's caul by the midwife, who wanted to give it to a sailor friend. The mother preferred to keep it for her baby's good luck and refused the offer.

Our coven Fetch, Francis De'Venney, has a family tradition of seamanship and has himself been a trawlerman. He had a caul, but it was lost, possibly stolen, and he says he must get another.

He tells us, by the way, that, in addition to the practical reason for a sailor's wearing a gold ear-ring (to pay for his burial if his body is washed ashore), there is a belief that it is a charm against drowning – which looks like a case of double insurance. But if it is worn slightly higher on the ear-lobe, it is a charm against death by fire.

If you find a spider spinning a web in the house in the morning, particularly in a window, it means money is coming; but you must leave the web undisturbed till the money actually turns up. Then you may remove the web, but you must apologize to the spider for having to do so.

Spiders must never be killed; they have been good-luck symbols since pagan times, and in Christian and Muslim popular tradition. Their webs have been used since time immemorial to cover cuts and to cure ague, asthma, warts and insomnia.

A spell to protect a newborn child against evil spirits has been very widespread in geography and in time. It is known as the Couvade. It involves the father enacting childbirth – groaning when his wife groans and, after the birth, taking the child to his bed and behaving as though it were he who had gone through all the pains of confinement and was recovering from them. Friends and neighbours support this meticulous charade, giving him the appropriate foods, while the mother takes the child away only long enough to feed it.

The wand has always been a recognized tool of magicians, witches and fairy godmothers; but one kind has long been used magically by ordinary people, and that is the glass kind, with many internal hair lines or tiny coloured seeds. Hung up in a house, they are supposed to force any demon or malignant witch who enters to stop and count the lines or the seeds. This takes some time, and meanwhile he or she cannot harm anyone in the house. The wand is also said to absorb any illness or infection. Any harmful influences it has collected can be wiped away in the morning with a cloth.

The 'tool' for a sixteenth-century English spell, which is still waiting to be worked, hangs on the wall of Buckland Abbey near Plymouth. It is the drum which Sir Francis Drake is believed to have taken with him on his voyage round the world. The tradition is that when he lay dying, he ordered that the drum be taken back to Devon. If England was ever in danger, it should be struck, and he would come back to help defend her.

Or, if Devonshire legend is to be believed, this spell has already been worked at least twice – and Drake *has* come back, not in his own shape but reincarnated as the great Admirals Blake and Nelson. And there are persistent claims that his drum was heard during World War II on the eve of the Dunkirk evacuation, and again on the eve of D-Day – both, appropriately, maritime operations of vital importance to Drake's country.

In describing the popular spells and charms which we have sampled here and in the last three chapters, we have used the words 'is' and 'was' somewhat arbitrarily – because we have found that it is never possible to say with confidence that a particular folk-belief is dead. Such things have a remarkable survival capacity and crop up in the most unexpected quarters.

These spells and charms obviously vary in quality, but to dismiss them all can be just as unwise as naïvely to accept them all.

An example of over-confident dismissal. Edward Jenner, as a teenager, knew of a Gloucestershire folk-belief that people who were infected by cowpox from cattle became immune from smallpox. Physicians of the time despised this belief as superstition, so when Jenner began experimenting, he at first kept quiet about it for fear of professional ridicule. He went ahead to discover vaccination, which completely confirmed the folk 'superstition' – and virtually wiped out the scourge of smallpox.

Some spells, charms and folk-beliefs are indeed mere superstition, while others contain precious buried truths. But which of them?

One thing is certain: to answer that question, we must not brush them aside or let them be lost but must treasure them and strive to understand them, in terms of our awareness of multi-level reality.

As one American, speaking to an Amazon tribe whose way of life was threatened with extinction, put it: 'Every time an old medicine man dies, it is as though a whole library were burned down.'

# XV  *Healing Spells*

In the various contexts of the earlier chapters, we have quoted many healing spells already; now let us look at the subject itself.

On healing spells, and psychic healing in general, one point should be strongly emphasized. It is wrong and very dangerous to regard such work as being in rivalry with, or contemptuous of, 'normal' medical treatment; the two should complement each other.

All too often we find that people who ask us for healing work are too afraid, or too lazy, to go to the doctor. So our first reaction to healing requests is always to ask: 'What does your doctor say?' – and then to make sure our treatment supports, and does not conflict with, the doctor's treatment; or if we find the patient has not consulted a doctor and there is the slightest indication that it would be advisable, to see that he or she does.

Two things should be remembered. First, many doctors and nurses were attracted to their profession in the first place because consciously or unconsciously, they have a natural healing ability. We have all met

GPs and nurses whose very involvement in a case is as therapeutic as their pills. And second, while one should listen to one's intuition in diagnosis, it is dangerously arrogant to assume it can always replace years of medical training. A good doctor relies on both.

We have had nurses, doctors and other medical workers in our coven, and we know of many others in the Craft. Andraste of San Francisco, for example, works as an assistant to a physician and tells us that, ' ... frequently patients ask for spells or herbal adjuncts to more standard treatments'. You will notice she is wise enough to say 'adjuncts' – and we are sure she is an asset to her employer.

Most people who use healing spells have their own preferred techniques.

Susa Morgan Black tells us that, in healing spells,

> Stones are my favourite method of using colour. Green stones are wonderful general healing tonics, yellow stones are great mental stimulants, red stones are good blood purifiers and energizers, blue stones can help with memory, purple stones can enhance spirituality.
>
> If you have a friend with a chronic heart problem, make a poppet of that person, and insert a fine piece of rose quartz in the heart area of the doll.
>
> If a friend has a broken leg, have a picture of that person, whole and healthy, on your altar with a piece of clear quartz on the leg. Use this to send healing energy to your friend.
>
> Colour is a wonderful way to heal. You can have people who are emotionally traumatized wear pink stones or pink clothes; have them drink water that has been charged by rose quartz overnight (especially during full Moon); give them a pink treatment, using pink cellophane over a light source, and shining it on their bodies as you massage them.

The use of stones and gems for colour healing overlaps, of course, with the resonance effect we discussed on p. 40.

Colour also enters into the use of candles. We and many others find candles an effective method of concentration in spell-working; you can intensify your awareness of the purpose as you light and gaze at the flame, which in itself delivers a message of concentrated focus and intensity of will-power. And the feeling of sustained effort is heightened by declaring that the purpose will have been achieved either by the time the candle has burned down to a needle stuck in its side or when it has burned out altogether, whichever feels appropriate.

'Laying-on of hands' is a familiar method of psychic or spiritual healing. It is somewhat outside the field of spell-working as such, but it may well enter into both diagnosis and the spell itself as an accessory, so to speak.

On this point, one fact is worth knowing: that everyone has an energy-giving and an energy-receiving hand. For most people, the right hand is the 'giver' – but these are not necessarily the same people as those who are customarily right-handed in other ways.

Here is a simple way to find out. Clasp your two hands together naturally, with the fingers intertwined. (Everyone instinctively does this in his or her own way, and finds the other way awkward.) The hand with the thumb on top is your energy-giving hand, better for emphasizing the action of a healing spell. The other hand is your energy-receiving one, better for diagnosis or for drawing off negative energy.

An important thing to remember here, though: if you are drawing off negative energy, every few seconds you should hold your hand off to one side and shake it free of the energy (making sure that there is no person or animal nearby in that direction). Otherwise you may absorb the harmful energy yourself.

Many healing spells from ancient times, and from other lands, will be found in Chapters XI and XV, but here are a couple to end this chapter.

First, a Chaldaean spell to cure headache. A band of cords, with a knot on the right, is arranged flat and regular with 'a woman's diadem' on the left. The instructions continue:

> Divide it twice into seven smaller bands;
> Wind it around the head of the sick one;
> Wind it around his seat of life;
> Wind it around his hands and his feet;
> Seat him on his bed
> And anoint him with charmed waters.

And an Ancient Egyptian spell to cure snakebite. It is recited over a model of a hawk (representing the god Horus), made of ivy-wood and painted, with two feathers on its head. You open its mouth and offer it bread, beer and incense and then put it on the patient's face and recite:

Flow out, thou poison, come forth upon the ground. Horus conjures thee, he cuts thee off, he spits thee out, and thou risest not up but fallest down. Thou art weak and not strong, a coward and dost not fight, blind and dost not see. Thou liftest not thy face. Thou art turned back and findest not thy way. Thou mournest and dost not rejoice. Thou creepest away and dost not appear. So speaketh Horus, efficacious of magic! The poison which was rejoicing, the hearts of multitudes grieve for it; Horus hath slain it by his magic. He who mourned is in joy. Stand up, thou who wast prostrate. Horus hath restored thee to life. He who came as one carried is gone forth of himself. Horus hath overcome his bites. All men, when they behold Ra, praise the son of Osiris. Turn back, thou snake, conjured is thy poison which was in any limb of [name] the son of [name]. Behold, the magic of Horus is powerful against thee. Flow out, thou poison, forth upon the ground.

# XVI  *Love Spells*

In popular belief, love spells are high on the agenda of a witch's activities. The incantation, or the mysterious potion, which will bring tall-dark-and-handsome to your doorstep with a bunch of roses in his hand and his wallet stuffed with credit cards; or the ice-maiden suddenly thawing and leaping into your bed, all others forgotten.

We have suffered from the effects of this belief, as have most witches. The petitioner has faith that the witch can bypass the desired one's freedom of choice (not to mention the petitioner's own shortcomings) and have them both living happily ever after.

In some cases, not even ever after. One man rang us up offering us £100 if we could get a particular lady into bed with him. Stewart, who took the call, began to explain our attitude to such requests, and the man interrupted, as though in mitigation, by explaining: 'Only for one night.' He was most offended when Stewart abandoned diplomacy and told him what he thought of him.

To be fair, most requests are more sincere than that one. Many petitioners genuinely believe they can consolidate happiness if only the initial hurdles can be overcome; and maybe some of them are right. But the basic ethical problem of whether a spell is justified is seldom as simple as they seem to think.

In their issue of 15 July 1988, *Best* magazine ran an article 'Witchcraft – Is It Really So Wicked?', for which they had interviewed several people, including ourselves. It was a very sensible and balanced article, at which no reasonable witch could complain. (It even included a Catholic expert on minority religious groups, Jackie Clackson, who said she found that witches ' ... seem to be caring about others and about ecology and have a feeling for nature and natural healing. I've met a few and feel, as a Christian, I'm speaking the same language.' She merely considered – as she was entitled to do – that, although she found that 'on the whole, witches are more religious than most people', they did not go far enough.)

On love spells, the article quoted Janet as follows: 'Some people do love spells using wax images. Personally, I think they're a bit iffy, but they do work. I could get a girl the lover she was after in 24 hours, but the problem is what happens when she doesn't want him any more? A lover brought to you by magic won't be so easy to get rid of.'

In fact, Janet had given more reasons for the 'iffy-ness' of love spells, but in a two-page article the magazine understandably couldn't quote everybody in full. But, as a result, we were snowed under with letters from people begging us to work love spells for them. Some of them clearly hadn't read beyond the words '24 hours'. At the time of writing this, it is a month or more since the article appeared, and we are still wading through, trying to answer them.

One of them we cannot resist quoting. It was from a 20-year-old girl who said: 'I have decided upon the man I want to marry. It is Michael Jackson the singer. However, my prospects of meeting him are slim. I wonder if you could devise a spell that would inflame his desire and make him fall in love with me?'

We can reassure Mr Jackson that we took no such action!

Some of these requests are moving, some pathetic and some transparently selfish. To many, we can give the kind of purely human advice a psychologist, social worker or sympathetic friend could give; but as far as actual spells are concerned, for virtually all of them we have to explain why these are out of the question.

In the first place, it would be wrong to work such a spell when one has not met, and had time to get to know, both of the people concerned (and, in some cases, third parties as well). Otherwise one has heard only one side of things, possibly inadequately at that, and simply cannot judge the situation fairly.

But the basic ethical problem is: would such a spell amount to manipulation? Would it distort or nullify the individual's freedom of judgement and action? As we saw in Chapter III, such manipulation is not only morally impermissible, it is highly dangerous.

A manipulative love spell is even more dangerous, perhaps, than most forms of manipulation. Real love involves all the levels, including the conscious mind, the intuitive mind, the emotions and the body. Its balance is more complex and subtle than any other sphere of human functioning, and it must find its own level – helped at most by understanding advice, encouragement or warnings, but even such help must be restrained and cautious.

A love spell which rides roughshod over the natural balance, and over freedom of choice, may indeed work to begin with. But inevitably the natural balance will reassert itself in the end, and the results will almost certainly be disastrous for both parties – and for the person who irresponsibly worked the spell.

Is a love spell never justified, then?

It can be – but only to help remove obstacles to a natural development; and its purpose must be very exactly envisaged, as, of course, must that of any spell. It must include the firmly held, and willed, proviso – ' ... but only if it is right for them both.'

An example from years back, when we were living in London. Janet had watched two friends who were clearly attracted to each other, but both of them were much too shy to make the first move. After a while Janet decided that help was both needed and justified. So she took two chess pieces, a king and a queen, identified them with the man and the woman and put them at opposite ends of the mantelpiece. Each day she moved them nearer together, willing the obstacles to be overcome – ' ... but only if it is right for them'. Neither of them knew of her action, then or since; but very soon the man plucked up his courage and asked the girl for a date.

Their relationship blossomed, they married, and when we last heard they were very happily raising a family.

There is a subtle point here about the designing of spells, but an important one. Janet moved the two chess pieces by equal amounts towards each other – not just one towards the other. Just moving one would have implied that only one of them needed to adjust to the situation, whereas, in the development of any love relationship, neither must remain static and embattled – in other words, manipulative. Who actually makes the breakthrough is up to them, but the underlying movement must be mutual. If Janet had moved only one, her psychological attitude to the problem would have been wrong, and in spell-working the psychological attitude is all-important.

Time and again it is really the applicant, rather than the object of his or her desire, who needs to be worked on. One witch we know was constantly pestered by an acquaintance to work love spells for her. Having no illusions about the woman, our friend consistently refused. In the end the woman got hold of a popular book of spells and worked her own, fuelling it with her own powerful desire. It worked – time and again – but in each case, as soon as she had bedded a man, she no longer wanted him. Her motivation was sexual only, indifferent to the men as people; she merely wanted to dominate and use them. Our witch friend had warned her that this would happen, but she took no notice.

There are too many people around like this woman, in the grip of their emotions, who would ignore all warnings, all ethical factors, and try to use love spells to achieve their ends.

The most effective, and justifiable, love spell of all is the one you work on yourself.

Susa Morgan Black of San Francisco has the right idea. She tells us: 'I don't believe in doing a love spell for a particular person. I believe in being specific about what you are looking for in a man or woman, and including that in the spell. Then, let go and enjoy your life. Be patient and trust your higher self and the gods.'

This certainly worked for Susa: 'I created sacred space, with candles and incense, and anointed my magic mirror with mugwort oil. [Mugwort is a herb of Venus.] I looked deep into the mirror and projected my image into the astral, to the unknown man in my future, my soul mate. My intention was to draw him to me by entering his dreams and make him long to meet me. Strangely enough, when I met Michael, I looked familiar to him, although we had never met before.'

Out of interest, Susa has collected together a Love Magic Museum, which ' ... contains charms and talismans of all sorts. I have Welsh love spoons, all sorts of love-drawing herbs and stones, Adam and Eve roots, mojo bags, poppets, wicker charms, love magnets, love-drawing candles, oils and incenses, etc.' Doubtless the original owners of many of these things would have used them in ways of which Susa would have disapproved!

Kevin Carlyon of Sussex tells us how he met his wife Ingrid as an unexpected result of a piece of working he had done for quite a different purpose. He quotes it to illustrate the importance of controlling one's extraneous thoughts during spell-working. If this is not done, thoughts irrelevant to the intention of the spell can steal power from it and produce unintended manifestations. In this case, Kevin was lucky – the side-effect was entirely positive; but if his extraneous thoughts had been negative, so might the result have been.

A local occult shop in Hastings [he tells us] asked me to make a special candle to bring luck to the business. Carrissa who owned the shop had designed her own set of Tarot cards, so I thought it would be good to etch the design of one of them on to a candle. I chose the Star card.

I charged it with positive energy; but I realized that, while making the candle, I had been thinking about personal things also – one of which was to find a new girl friend, as I didn't have one at the time.

I took the candle to the shop, and Carrissa was delighted with it. About a week later I was at an occult fair in Hastings when I noticed a girl reading a book on witchcraft. The owner of the stall was trying to sell her what I considered to be rubbish, so I went over and recommended your book *The Witches' Way*.

We chatted, and started going out together. About a week later, I went to her flat, and there I saw the Star candle which I had made. It turned out Carrissa's mother had sold it to Ingrid by accident ... The rest, as they say, is history.

Helen from Lancashire gives us another example of the principle that, in matters of love, it is usually the seeker, not the sought-after, who needs working on. She is the eldest of three sisters. In 1981 she worried about the middle sister, who

... due to personal, medical and social reasons had reached the age of twenty-five without ever having had a boy friend. This was exacerbated by the fact that I had been married for seven years, and our younger sister had a constant stream of admirers.

We decided to help. We pricked a pentagram on a new candle, anointed it and charged it with the idea of more self-confidence for my sister, especially in the area of romance.

We had to put the candle somewhere where she would pass over it daily, but my mother wouldn't find it while she was cleaning! In the end, I pushed it through the loose weave of the fabric on the underside of her divan bed. (As far as I know, it is still there!)

Anyway, the spell did its work. My sister's social life suddenly blossomed, and within two years she was married – and has lived happily ever after.

Sex, as we saw in Chapter VII, is one of the strongest psychic power-sources in the human make-up. As part of a many-level loving relationship, it can be a glowing jewel. As a sole motivation, it can be a bull in the human china-shop, and any relationship which tries to found itself on that alone is heading at best for a disappointing fade-out, and at worst for serious mutual damage.

If a loving relationship already exists, even at an early stage of development, there is no harm at all in using spells to enhance that development. But they should be worked on yourself, not on your partner. Realizing that it is you as a person the partner loves, you should try to see yourself through his or her eyes, to understand what in particular he or she loves, and strive to develop it – but without falsifying your basic nature, which would defeat the object of the exercise.

One of the best love spells of this nature is the simple word 'Sorry' – the frank admission that you have failed or hurt your partner in some way and that you are not too proud to say so or to try to put it right. (It often evokes the response, 'No, it was my fault too' – which is a step forward for both of you, though you should neither expect nor demand it, or your 'Sorry' is only half meant.) It may sound an over-statement to call this a 'spell', but a spell it is – because, if it is sincere, it is not merely an apology, it is an undertaking to yourself that you will try not to repeat the mistake; and in committing yourself to being bound by that undertaking, you are indeed working a spell on yourself.

Material aids and symbols, as we have seen elsewhere, can be of great help in spell-working, by providing a focus for your imagination and will-power. They can be helpful in this context, too.

Say, for example, that you know your partner values your calmness and depends on it to balance his or her own nervousness or tendency to over-reaction. You know, then, that this is a quality worth strengthening, if only for love of your partner. So when you are alone, you could take a candle, of one of the appropriate colours (see p. 45), relax and light it. Then tell yourself something like this: 'That candle is my gift of calmness. It burns with my love, ardent but not scorching. Its light is bright but not blinding. Its flame burns steadily. If a draught disturbs it, it returns quickly to its natural shape. If something blows it out, I can relight it in an instant. It is a bright star in the darkness, and the deeper the dark, the more my lover needs it to find his/her way. I must make sure it is always alight when he/she needs it ...'

And so on, searching your mind for more parallels between the candle and the calmness which your partner values; why it is the colour it is, for example, or why you are burning it in a particular candlestick. Keep the candle in a safe place, and take it out and repeat your solitary meditation on it whenever you feel the need. Before long, when you feel your calmness threatened, merely conjuring up the mental image of the candle-flame should be quite enough to restore it.

It is a good idea (as with all spells) to use your ingenuity to find symbols which mean something to you. So here is an exercise.

Say you know you are prone to jealousy, and that it is harming your relationship. Here are some statements you might make to yourself:

'Jealousy is a bad smell. It makes the home less of a home.'

'Jealousy means lack of confidence in myself; I fear that other people may be more attractive or interesting than I am.'

'Jealousy is possessiveness. My lover and I are willing partners, people in our own right, not each other's property. Possessiveness is not love.'

'Jealousy can eat away the precious shared moments, whether of peace or of passion. It is a poison to be eradicated.'

'Jealousy is green because mould and decay are green.'

And so on and so on. Try working out symbols and simple rituals for banishing it – or whatever other fault you know needs dealing with.

A spell to protect a loved one and to keep him or her aware of, and reassured by, the links with the love at the home base while he or she is away, is sent to us by Laurie Cabot of Salem, Massachusetts. Laurie, by the way, is known as 'The Official Witch of Salem' – a complimentary title bestowed on her by Governor Michael Dukakis, whose name is not unknown even to non-American readers.

For her spell, you need a needle, a pink candle, a black candle, an incense-burner, frankincense and myrrh, a large jar with a tight lid, some black velvet, a pure gold pentacle and some black thread. (A 'pure gold pentacle' is something few witches will possess; we certainly don't. But any gold disc or coin, however small, will serve the purpose, as long as you designate and envisage it as a bearing the essence of a five-pointed star, even if the star is invisible.)

Laurie writes:

Place the ingredients on your table or altar. Cast a Magic Circle. Burn the incense to purify your Circle. Then light the black candle to draw in all the energy to cast the spell, and the pink candle for love. Wrap the pentacle in black velvet, and sew it around to cover it.

Add two strings of black thread long enough to put over the rim of the glass jar.

Hold the wrapped pentacle in your left hand, and cover it with your right hand. Close your eyes, and in your mind's eye visualize your loved one. Then as the candles flicker and the incense clouds the room, say aloud:

> A golden ring around a star
> Placed in black velvet
> And hung in a jar
> Will keep you, my love,
> While you are afar.
> I ask that all of this may be correct
> And for the good of all.
> So mote it be.

Then put the covered pentacle in the jar and close the lid. Find a place to keep the jar up high on a shelf, or hang it from a ribbon over a door facing a window, on a nail or a plant-hanger out of reach.

Laurie tells us that when this spell was used in the case of a runaway child, the runaway phoned, saying, 'Mom, I'm coming home. I could feel your protection and love.'

On this kind of work – a pertinent thought from Maxine Sanders in her book *Maxine: The Witch Queen* (pp. 150–1):

> One can work what is called 'sympathetic' magic in these cases which is sometimes successful. 'Sympathetic' here means 'working in entire sympathy with', and very often this involves the use of images. Sympathy with the image created is absolutely necessary if you are to hope for any success in this form of magic. Perhaps it isn't realized how absolute this love, this sympathy, must be. This is what makes things so difficult for the black witch who may be working to kill. You must love the image you create as much as you would your own child, and if this love isn't there you are wasting your time. The black witch is caught between this clash of emotions – love for what she has created coupled with a death-wish. Not easy!

Or, as Spike Milligan put it: 'Kindness and love, that old-fashioned medicine, is still the best in the long run.'

Closely allied to such positive love spells are human fertility spells. Problems of human infertility should, of course, always first be taken to your doctor, in case there is anything mundanely practical that can be done. But time and again a couple may long for a child but fail to conceive one, even though the doctor can find no physical reason.

Two friends of Stewart's were in this position. They tried for years without success and finally resigned themselves to it, adopted a child and relaxed. A few months later, to their surprise, the wife conceived. Happy with their new two-child family, they used to joke about their luck, calling it 'the china egg syndrome'. (For readers unfamiliar with poultry: china eggs are sometimes put underneath hens to encourage them to lay real ones – and this often works.)

They are not the only such case we have heard of – which points to the fact that apparent infertility may often be psychosomatic, due to over-anxiety and tension. And psychosomatic problems are very responsive to psychic treatment (in a word, to spells) because they mean that more than one level of the total individuality is involved, and experience shows that they are best tackled from the 'inner' end.

How about a spell to overcome this problem of infertility through over-anxiety?

Take some clay or wax and make a little image of a pregnant woman, with full belly and breasts. Add something to identify it with the woman concerned – say, a snippet of her hair firmly attached to the head. Then, with the usual methods of precise formulation and vivid visualization, tell the image your intent. (This is best done if possible by the man and woman together.)

Then wrap it in a golden or yellow cloth, and find an appropriate Earth-Mother site in which to bury it. This could be a place of known magical power, such as a megalithic site or a healing well with a female patron such as Brighid; or even a church with a female patron saint. You should devote some careful thought and research to choosing this site. Of course, you must not bury it in the churchyard itself or do anything which desecrates your chosen site (whether megalithic or religious) in any way. That would be both illegal and offensive, and particularly in the case of archaeological sites could do irreparable damage. But you can certainly find a burying-spot which does not do this, yet is within the sphere of influence of the place's power.

Bury the image during the waxing Moon, telling it as you do so that you are putting it where it will be safe and handing over your problem to the Earth Mother. End with a plea to the Earth Mother herself, both for fertility and for the removal of tension and anxiety.

We know at least one couple who found such a ritual successful.

In the Middle Ages, love spells followed the general trend of using bits and pieces of animals – often unmistakably 'sympathetic' pieces. For example, from a collection entitled *The Boke of the Mervayles of the World*, a spell to keep your woman faithful to you: 'If though wilt that a woman bee not visious nor desire men, take the private members of a Wolfe, and the haires that doe grow on the cheekes or eyebrows of him, and haires that be under his beard, and burn it all, and give it to her to drinke, when she knoweth not, and she shall desire no other man.' One would think that 'when she knoweth not' would be the most difficult part, with such a concoction.

And a grimly kinky (not to mention sacrilegious) one from the *Grimorium Verum*: 'How to Make a Girl Dance in the Nude: Write on the virgin parchment the character of FRUTIMIERE with the blood of a bat. Then Cut it on a blessed stone, over which a Mass has been said. After this when you want to use it, place the character under the sill or threshold of a door which she must pass. When she comes past, she will come in. She will undress and be completely naked, and will dance unceasingly until death.' The *Grimorium* admits the self-defeating nature of this spell by adding: '... if one does not remove the character; with grimaces and contortions which cause more pity than desire'.

On a kindlier note, two little examples from our Christian friends.

We once visited a charming little church in Spain which had a statue of the Virgin in its Lady Chapel, richly gowned and jewelled with generations of local gifts and carrying a Jesus-doll in her lap. One little old man had the job of looking after them and keeping the gowns and jewels in proper condition.

After our visit, a friend told us the man's story. He and his wife had reached early middle age without the child they desperately wanted, so he went to the Virgin who was in his care and prayed earnestly to her. To their delight, his wife bore the baby they longed for.

In the natural course of events, he learned the details of baby-rearing, so he applied them to his church job. Daily thereafter, he undressed the Jesus-doll, attended to its bottom and carefully put on a clean nappy – in thankfulness to its mother for answering his prayer.

Gratitude to your gods (in whatever form you envisage them) for the success of your spells is something worth keeping in mind.

Nearer home, there is a Sister Marie Claire in Dublin who, we are told, is in the habit of telling newly-weds: 'And here's a little prayer for you: "Give me oil in my lamp and keep me burning all through the night." '

Which isn't a bad spell at all, at all.

# XVII   *Spells to Solve Problems*

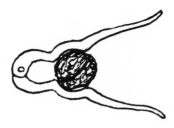

Money is high on the list of a lot of people's problems, and money spells are many and various. Everyone knows the one about turning over your money in your pocket when you see the New Moon through glass, so that it may increase with the waxing of the Moon.

Seldiy Bate of London reports another one, which she says should be worked on the first of the calendar month (doubtless a memory of another New Moon custom, for the first of the lunar month). 'Retrieve all the loose change in the house and from your pockets. When you leave the house for the first time on the first day of the month, open the front door, step over the threshold and then turn round and throw all the money back into the house. Leave it there until you return, when you should collect it all up and put it in a savings box, making sure to give some coins away next time you receive money.'

Such gestures of gratitude, or of acknowledgement to the gods who have been gracious enough to grant your wish, are common in folklore – and perhaps not too bad a habit for modern spell-workers to cultivate!

Which leads us to another money spell of Seldiy's, though it is sophisticated witchcraft magic rather than folklore. It is specifically for gold and should be worked, she says, at sunrise on a Sunday when the Moon is waxing.

You will need a gold or golden-yellow-coloured cloth; six gold-coloured candles; incense of Ra; and something made out of gold, no matter how small.

['Incense of Ra' is an incense which Seldiy makes herself – see Appendix 3 under Acca and Adda. But failing that, any incense or joss-sticks which evoke the Sun, such as amber, will fit the bill.]

At the appropriate time, without speaking to anybody beforehand, prepare everything in silence, just before sunrise. You should work robed if you have a golden-yellow robe, otherwise skyclad.

Set out a simple altar, facing East or South, draped with the gold-coloured cloth. Have the incense ready to burn. Set out the six candles in a circle equally spaced (with one at the topmost point as you look at the altar).

Place the gold object in the centre of the circle of candles. When you are ready to begin, burn a little of the incense and breathe in the perfume, allowing it to activate the magical centres of the body (chakras).

Now light the six candles, starting with the topmost one and continuing deosil (clockwise). As the light increases, sense golden light filling the space where you are working.

Continue to breathe the sense of golden light building up, and put a generous amount of incense into your burner. As the smoke rises, visualize your thoughts reaching up towards the rising Sun and visualize gold pouring into the centre of the circle of candles and into the gold object, magnifying it.

Now take the gold object out of the circle of candles and hold it in both hands. As you clasp it, feel the energy of golden light permeating through your body.

Now blow the candles out as your visualization culminates as the flames go out; let the energy of the extinguished flames solidify your mental image.

Give thanks and put all away. You should keep the candles and then burn them right down when your goal has been achieved. You should carry your small piece of gold with you (or put it somewhere relevant) in order for it to attract more gold.

Keep silent about this working. Gold will come to you.

Magic will always work if the rules have been obeyed and if your motives are pure. Remember that everything is symbolic. The day after I worked this spell, a grateful client who had been helped by my advice sent me a magnificent bouquet of golden-yellow flowers!'

Theatre ushers have a money spell of their own. Many believe you should not spend the first tip you receive in a new run but should rub it against your legs and then keep it in your pocket throughout the run. This will ensure that there will be plenty more. (Incidentally, they believe it unlucky to accept a tip from a woman buying a programme, but safe to do so from a man; lucky to seat the first playgoer to arrive for any performance, unless the ticket is numbered 13; unlucky not to hear the first words of the play; and unlucky if a woman faints in your section.)

Lady Isis of Columbus, Ohio, contributes a spell which

> ... can be varied in many different ways for whatever your purpose. Here is how it can be used to see if you will get a job promotion.
>
> On a piece of parchment paper, in green ink, using a dip pen, write your name, birth date, address, lucky number, zodiac sign, etc. etc., and your desire for this job promotion. Write with all the feeling and emotion you can muster.
>
> On the other side of the paper, in red ink, write your boss's name, department, position, description, etc. – all the information you know about him/her.
>
> Roll the paper into a scroll, and tie with a piece of white string. Place the scroll in a bottle of plain clear water, and cap tightly. Let it stand a few hours or overnight, then remove the scroll.
>
> Examine the string carefully. If the string is green, you have a good chance to obtain your desire. If the string is red, then your desire is not yet meant to be. If the string remains white, put more emotion into the making of it next time.

(And, one might add, make sure your string isn't non-absorbent nylon!)

Another spell to help a job-seeker. Take some honey – from your own hive is ideal, or the home-collected kind you find on market stalls; otherwise a commercial jar will do (of clear honey, because you want the intention to be clear, not cloudy). Make little pastry tart-cases, fill them with honey, cover them with more pastry like mince pies and cook them. Ritually bless them for the person you are helping, with the verse:

> Your life shall be like the honey-bee,
> A happy hive of industry.
> Work for you there soon will be.
> In the name of the Old Ones, so mote it be!

Then simply give them to your friend, telling him or her to eat one and crumble one outside for the birds, each day. Most baking-tins are for a dozen, which will last six days; starting on a Monday might be a good idea, as an extra touch of sympathetic magic, because that is when most working weeks start.

Susa Morgan Black, who, as we saw in Chapter XV, uses crystals in healing spells, also finds them effective as problem-solvers:

Create a sacred space for yourself by placing three crystals in a triangle around you. Hold another crystal in your hand, and clear your mind. You might also want to wear crystal on your head, as in earrings or a circlet around your head. Affirm that your mind is clear, and a perfect channel for the information that you need. Your mind may start to sparkle, feel charged, and thoughts will pour through it! You may even have to slow your thinking down to filter all the information you will receive. In that state of mind, the options will be revealed.

Ty Dawson finds that a useful focus for a problem-solving spell is to take one of the Tarot Major Arcana 'synonymous with the problem or situation it is hoped to affect'. Concentrated meditation on the Tarot image is directed towards producing an appropriate thought-form. 'It is best used when an important decision is to be made, when there are two equally balanced options on offer.' It seems that, ' ... the archetypal imagery of a Tarot trump really does awaken the inner voice, that hidden twin self that always points us in the right direction.'

Seldiy Bate has a spell for finding a lost object:

Write down a description of the object on a piece of paper. Take a long pin, like a dressmaking pin or a hatpin. Last thing at night, before retiring, energize the pin by stroking your fingers along it eight times, while repeating the name of the lost object. Take the piece of paper and pin it energetically to the sofa. Leave the paper there till you find what you have lost.

This traditional custom is called 'Pinning the Devil' and is very old indeed; it has been in my family for generations.

It works even better if you use parchment and a burin (engraving-tool) – although if you have no sofa, you must have lost it, and I can only suggest pinning your request for the lost sofa to a cushion!

If the missing 'object' is a pet, Seldiy has a spell for that too:

Take a length of fine green ribbon and lay it in a circle around something belonging to your pet – preferably its bed or home. Add a photograph, some fur, feather or scales, if you can – anything to create the psychic link. Call your pet by name into the circle, and then knot the ribbon with a threefold knot. Leave it set up like that till your pet returns.

It is advisable to burn some incense of an appropriate nature while visualizing your pet as you call it – Bast for cats, Selene for dogs, Hermes for birds and reptiles, and Pan for any animal. Don't forget to give thanks to the appropriate department when your pet returns. Making a donation to an animal charity would be an appropriate gesture.

(Seldiy, as we said above, always has the 'appropriate' incense to hand, because she makes them herself.)

One problem familiar to families with young children is that of sibling-jealousy when the second baby arrives. A good idea is to give the first child a welcoming spell to work which can help to implant a positive attitude in him or her from the start.

When the new baby is almost due, give the child a little potted plant that will survive in the garden (or even a window-box if you haven't a garden) and a trowel. With your help if necessary, get him or her to dig a hole and plant it and to recite at the same time:

> First Mummy and Daddy,
> And then they had me.
> First they were two,
> Then we were three.
> I plant this flower for you, baby.
> Welcome to our family!

It will be advisable to keep a discreet eye on the plant from then on, to make sure it thrives!

Finally, if your problem is 'You can't take it with you', we cannot resist quoting an item from the newsletter of the Toronto-based Pagans for Peace network:

WISH YOU WERE BORN RICH!!?? NOW YOU CAN BE!

Here's a Once in a Lifetime offer! First, leave You Were Born Rich $10,000 or more in your will. After you pass away, our professional medium will contact your spirit in the other world. Then you tell us when you're coming back and under what name. Upon your return we will regress you, at age 21, through his lifetime and ask you for your seven-digit account number.

Once you give us the number, we'll give you a cheque for your original investment plus interest. The longer you're gone, the more you will receive!! You may come back to find yourself a billionaire! Show your future self how much you care – leave a generous 'welcome back' present. We'll take care of the rest.

Before anyone rich and gullible rushes to reply, we should add that, while Pagans for Peace is a serious and genuine movement, its leader, Sam Wagar, has a healthy sense of humour.

# XVIII  *Weather Spells*

Weather is not only affectable by spells – it can itself affect them, in two ways. The psychic atmosphere is particularly sensitive to weather; and individuals differ greatly in their reactions to it.

Ty Dawson, for example, tells us that, 'Personally I have found the psychic awareness required during spell-magic, meditation or power-raising heightened during thunderstorms.' She is a writer and finds ' ... a greater flow in my work, and more inspiration, during storms, particularly those with concentrated lightning'. This, she feels, ' ... emphasizes the links between the human organism on all levels and the Earth organism itself'.

Ty is right; and the effect of those links varies from one individual to another. We ourselves, for example, find that high winds disturb Janet but exhilarate Stewart; yet both of us are uplifted, and made more psychically sensitive, by a clear starlit night sky.

A traditional maritime weather-spell comes from John the Sailor: 'A coin flung to windward on leaving harbour will buy a fair wind for day or two; but to be effective, it must be a coin that someone has dropped on deck by accident, and someone else has found. I don't usually use this, but a friend I have sailed with does, and it works.'

John himself doesn't feel justified in using weather spells:

> I have a strong feeling that there is a balance, which I am very wary of upsetting. Fair winds in my part of the ocean could be storm and rain a hundred miles down the coast ... I prefer to trust to my feel for the elements, and my skill with boats, such as it is. I don't think the Goddess is displeased with me; it's remarkable how often I get a fair slant of wind, or an opening in the visibility, just when I need it.

Many weather folk-spells, admittedly, seem merely concerned with pushing the bad weather somewhere else. Like the Scottish one:

> Rainy, rainy rattle-stanes,
> Dinna rain on me.
> Rain on John O'Groatie's hoose,
> Far across the sea

... which is rough on John O'Groats – and incidentally puzzling, for his famous house is on the shore, the most northerly building in mainland Scotland. But its extreme coastal isolation doubtless identified it in some people's minds with 'far across the sea'. (Irrelevant but interesting note: the pub which now stands beside it has the most extensive selection of Scotch whisky brands we have ever seen in one place.)

In ancient times (and in many tribal areas such as still exist in Africa or Australia today) this problem of inconveniencing neighbours did not arise because weather magic was on behalf of the whole community. Ancient Egypt (and modern, till the building of the Aswan Dam) was entirely dependent on the annual Nile inundation, which flooded and fertilized the riverside fields which were, and still are, the whole of Egypt's agriculture with the exception of a few oases. The adequacy of this inundation, as both rulers and people must have known, depended upon the year's rainfall hundreds of miles upstream, so the appropriate fertility magic was in effect weather magic.

In the centuries when Egypt's capital was Thebes (the modern Karnak and Luxor), the great magical ritual for this purpose was the annual Festival of Opet. Opet (Apet, Taueret) was the hippopotamus goddess of childbirth, and her festival marked the impregnation of Thebes' Earth-Mother goddess, Mut, by her consort Amun-Ra.

Another goddess involved was Sopdet, the Dog Star Sirius, more commonly known by her Greek name, Sothis. The Festival of Opet was held at 'the going-up of the goddess Sothis' – the heliacal rising of Sirius, which can be pinpointed exactly as 19 July by the modern calendar. It involved the ritual ferrying of Amun-Ra from his great temple at Karnak the few miles upstream to Mut's temple at Luxor, so that he could unite with her.

This was a case of the *hieros gamos* we explained on p. 53. A high priest would personify the god, and a young virgin priestess the goddess; and their ritual intercourse was the honeymoon of Amun-Ra and Mut by which the Earth Mother was made fertile.

Did this great public ritual, the popular rejoicing which accompanied it, and the *hieros gamos* which climaxed it really affect the rainfall of the Upper Nile? It is up to you to think what you will, but it can certainly be argued that the communal respect for Mother Earth which it involved, and the joyful celebration of her fertilizing, represented a healthier attitude towards her than some which are evident in today's exploitation of her.

As Doreen Valiente puts it (*Natural Magic*, p. 125): 'Such festivals arose from a deep, instinctive feeling of the oneness of all life. This instinct was the foundation of primitive religion and magic, coupled as it was with the idea that life itself flowed from an unseen divine source, from which all things came and to which all things would eventually return.'

Some people can, consciously or involuntarily, affect the weather of their immediate environment. We know one witch in the English Midlands who was feeling almost suffocated by a summer heat-wave and found herself wishing spontaneously but vehemently for a snowstorm to relieve it. The snowstorm happened – briefly and locally but enough in such 'freak' circumstances to make headlines in the town's newspaper. (That lady had to be very careful with her wishes; she found, for instance, that if she was angry with her next-door neighbour – a rather tiresome individual – his car would fail to start.)

As for deliberate wishes, one of our witches, the late Kathy De'Ath, had her own personal weather spell to invoke sunshine. She would buy potted marigolds, plant them in her garden and tell them that they were children of the Sun and that as long as they kept their eyes open for Daddy he would appear and watch them; otherwise he might veil himself.

Our coven Maiden, Ginny, has a spell she uses when the sky is patchy. She recites over and over:

> Patches of blue in the sky, dear,
> Patches of blue in the sky;
> Gather them up and sew them together,
> And soon we will have a change in the weather.

Ginny claims – as did Kathy with her marigold spell – that it usually works. Incidentally, Ginny sometimes also uses this same jingle in a metaphorical sense, to correct emotional 'patchy weather' (with the corresponding change in awareness of intent), and finds that this too works.

A traditional Sun-invoking spell uses an orange candle in a green candlestick – orange representing the Sun, and green the Earth beneath it. You stroke the candle downwards again and again, willing the power of the Sun into it. When you feel ready, you light the candle and leave it to burn itself out, as an invitation to the Sun to pour its own light upon the Earth.

Back to the sea. Witches have always had the reputation of being able to whistle up a wind, whether favourable for good sailing or violent to sink a ship. If a sailor knew a witch who was kindly disposed to him, he could even buy from her a measure of control over the strength of the wind. From Doreen Valiente again (*ibid.*, p. 131): 'A widespread belief in the islands of Scotland and the Isle of Man was that witches could sell winds to sailors by means of the charm of a knotted cord. The cord had three knots in it, one for a light breeze, two for a strong wind and three for a gale. The sailor had to undo the knots when out at sea and the wind would blow as required.'

Finnish witches were said to use the same method. According to Richard Eden, writing in 1577, 'They tie three knots on a string hanging on a whip. When they loose one of these, they raise tolerable winds. When they loose another, the wind is more vehement. But by loosing the third, they raise plain tempests, as in old time they were accustomed to raise thunder and lightning.'

Fear of the ability of witches to whistle up winds may well have lain behind the old rhyme:

> A whistling woman and a crowing hen
> Are neither good for God nor men

During the hysteria of the witch persecution, far more bizarre methods than a mere whistle or knot-tying were attributed to them. The North Berwick witches, at their trial in 1590, were accused among other things of raising a storm to harm King James VI of Scotland (later James I of England) when he sailed to Norway to collect his fifteen-year-old queen, Anne of Denmark. James himself took part in their questioning in Holyrood Castle and forced the court to rescind its acquittal of one of them.

After prolonged torture, the principal accused, Agnes Sampson, admitted to having conjured up the storm by baptizing a cat, attaching 'the chiefest part of a dead man and several joints of his body' to each of its paws and throwing it in the sea. When she had confessed to this and fifty-two other charges, the torture stopped and she was strangled and burned. (It is ironic, and typical of the times, that most of those fifty-three charges for which she was burned concerned healing the sick by charms!)

At least one other sovereign was prepared to take advantage of witches' power over the weather. When the King of Sweden was at war with the Danes in 1563, he included four witches in his staff to help give him favourable weather conditions.

The ability of witches to work weather spells was generally accepted knowledge. About 700, Archbishop Theodore of Canterbury ordained, in his *Liber Poenitentialis*, Article 21, a punishment of five years penance, one of them on bread and water, for the magical raising of storms; and half a millennium later, so distinguished a Church thinker as St Thomas Aquinas accepted this ability as fact.

Among the mentioned methods of raising storms, producing rain or otherwise affecting the weather were: beating the water of a pond with a rod; digging a hole and pouring water or urinating in it; throwing a sacrificed pullet into the air; throwing a flint over the left shoulder towards the West; throwing sea sand into the air; wetting a broom and shaking it; boiling hog bristles; laying sticks on a dry river bank; burying sage till it rotted; boiling eggs in a pail; beating a wet rag against a stone; or boiling a baby in a cauldron.

(This last one would either be crude anti-witch propaganda or a code used by the witches themselves for something harmless – a ploy witches and magicians sometimes used to frighten people off from probing into trade secrets ... An animal-rights enthusiast told a friend of ours, with appropriate horror, that 'The Sorcerer's Apprentice' occult supply shop in Leeds was selling the blood of lizards! Our friend was able to reassure him that 'dragon's blood' – the actual name – is, in fact, a resin of the palm tree *Calimus draco*, used as an ingredient in some incenses and for staining violins.)

There is, fortunately, no need to drown a cat, whether baptized or not, or sacrifice a pullet to affect the weather. Several Far Eastern peoples make use of a cat without drowning or killing it, merely making it wet or temporarily tying it up, to conjure up rain. In Sumatra, women carry a cat into the water and make it swim. The Javanese bathe a cat and then carry it round in procession. In the Celebes, they tie a cat to a chair and carry it round the fields that need rain. In Malaya, a woman will put a pot over her head upside down, then take it off, fill it with water and wash a cat in it till the unfortunate animal is thoroughly soaked.

We wondered why a cat was so popular for the purpose. One of our witches suggested that a cat symbolizes a rain cloud, in that, when the cat is heavily charged with water, it shakes itself so that the water flies off like raindrops. We pointed out that a dog does the same – but he in turn pointed out that a cat is easier to handle in this way than a dog!

At least you can explain your purpose to a human being, who can add his or her own will-power to the spell, which may be why the Druids conjured up rain by sprinkling a naked girl with water. Why always a female, and naked, some may ask? Obviously because she represented the Earth Mother whom the rain must fertilize; and she was naked because the unfertilized Earth is naked. Unlike the cat, she symbolized the recipient of the rain, not its source, and the spell was straightforward sympathetic magic. (Fortunately for her, in the latitudes where the Druids operated, it is in summer that rain is needed.)

The ancient Hebrews used to conjure up rain – in the name of the Lord, of course. Samuel declared: ' "Is it not the wheat harvest today? I will call unto the Lord, and he will send thunder and rain...." So Samuel called unto the Lord, and the Lord sent thunder and rain that day; and all the people greatly feared the Lord and Samuel' (I Samuel 12: 17–18).

Janet has found one simple method of influencing winds (moderate ones, in view of her aversion) to the state she wants. If she needs to increase a wind to dry her laundry, she stands with her back to it and exhales slowly, concentrating on that desired increase. If she wants to quieten it or to change its direction, she faces it and inhales and then either blows it back the way it came or exhales in the direction she wants it to blow – again with concentrated intent.

It used to be believed that cutting or burning ferns would bring on rain. When Charles I visited Staffordshire in 1636, his Chamberlain, Lord Pembroke, wrote beforehand to the High Sheriff of the county to ask that no ferns should be burned during the royal visit, to ensure fine weather.

Popular belief is that to open an umbrella in fine weather will bring rain. One wonders how the weather-gods know the difference between an umbrella and a parasol ... Umbrella folklore in Britain is only two centuries old, because umbrellas are a Chinese invention and did not appear in Britain till one Jonas Hanway ventured out with one in London in 1778, to be jeered at for his pains till its usefulness was appreciated. But at least the folklore itself is native, not imported, because in China the umbrella's symbology was very different – it could be used only by those of royal blood or those who had been honoured with royal permission.

A final recommendation on the subject of rain-making: read Chapter 5 of Elizabeth St George's *The Casebook of a Working Occultist* for an account of her husband's meeting in Nigeria with a witch-doctor who had studied science with her at Chelsea Polytechnic. Like the whole book, it makes hilarious reading but contains some very practical hints.

# XIX  *Binding Spells*

We hope we have established the point strongly enough by now that attacking-spells, or spells which attempt to manipulate someone against his or her will or natural development, are both unethical and dangerous to the spell-worker. We dealt with psychic defence in general in Chapter V, and with defence against known attack by use of the Boomerang Effect in Chapter IV.

But how about the situation where we know that someone is working evil – maybe not in the form of psychic attack or not against ourselves but against someone we feel we should help? It may not be practical to rely on the Boomerang Effect or to give the victim a crash course in psychic self-defence. Yet we are precluded from attacking the culprit. Must we then shrug our shoulders and leave the evil-doer with a free rein?

Not at all. Evil-doing can be checked without either counter-attack or manipulation, by a method known as a binding spell. This inhibits the culprit from harming anyone else, while consciously refraining from wishing any harm to himself or herself. In a sense it also evokes the Boomerang Effect, in that, if the culprit persists, that persistence will bounce back on its source. It may also – and even better – have the positive effect of making the culprit realize that the evil-doing is not working, and cause him or her to reconsider.

The most straightforward form of the binding spell involves the making, birthing and instructing of a wax or other image, as described on pp. 43–4. At the instructing phase, the image is told firmly what harm it (personifying its human subject) has been doing but from now on will be powerless to do. It must be told (phrasing it in your own words), 'We/I wish no harm on you yourself; any harm you suffer will be of your own making, so when you cease to inflict harm, you will escape it.' If a group or couple are working the spell, everyone taking part must voice the instructions, in his or her own way.

As with all image spells, you must use sustained imagination and will-power to identify the image with its human original, and be utterly confident that it provides an effective psychic link to that original.

The final stage is literally to bind the image, with black cord, and to wrap it in black cloth – black being the colour of restraint and the setting of boundaries. Concentration on the aim must be firmly maintained while this is being done, and preferably reinforced by repeating to the image why you are doing it. The wrapped image is then kept in a safe dark place until the aim of the working is achieved – not forgetting that, as soon as it is no longer needed, it must be ritually disposed of in running water as described on p. 44.

The image binding spell can be used by a solo worker, a couple or a group, but we have found it is a particularly effective way of co-ordinating and unifying a group effort.

For solo working, Robin Skelton (*The Practice of Witchcraft Today*) suggests a simpler equivalent of the image-binding – that is, to place a photograph of the subject before you and to have some black thread ready and a lit candle. You concentrate on the photograph, saying over and over again:

> I speak to you and bid you hear.
> I speak to you and bid you hear.

As you speak, you keep on breaking the thread in the candle flame. When you are confident that communication has been achieved, you instruct the photograph as you would the image. Finally you burn all the bits of the thread in the candle flame or the fire.

Robin Skelton recommends the same use of photograph (in this case, of the victim), candle and thread to break an obsessive bond which is doing somebody harm. In this case, the words spoken to the photograph are:

This is a bond and it is broken.
Of this bondage you are free.
By the power of the Lady,
As I will so must it be.

There is an equally simple method which we have also used with success. A young woman we knew and cared about greatly was being exploited and made unhappy by a man for his own transparently selfish ends. We simply wrote his name on a piece of paper, which we buried in our garden, declaring firmly: 'As this paper rots, so will he leave her alone.' Within a few weeks, he had done just that – unexpectedly from her point of view (she knew nothing of our working), but permanently.

There may be occasions, of course, when the culprit will be sensitive enough to identify the source of the binding and to attempt a counter-offensive, so you should look to your own psychic defence at the same time.

Susa Morgan Black's husband Michael devised his own form of binding spell to protect a friend who was under a heavy psychic attack: 'He placed the perpetrator in a green fog,' Susa tells us. 'The fog grounded all the negative energy this person was generating, so that rather than hurting our friend or anyone else, the energy just fell back to earth, for the Earth Goddess to transform and re-use positively. Michael added the *geis* that when this person no longer generated this negative energy, she could blow the fog away herself.' (*Geis* – pronounced 'gesh' – is an Irish Gaelic word meaning a command, obligation or prohibition laid on an individual by someone of power, whether official or magical. It occurs frequently in Irish mythology. The plural is *geasa*, pronounced 'gassa'.)

Talking of fog, actual meteorological fog also has the reputation of screening and grounding negative forces. (As does water – hence the old tradition, enshrined, for example, in Robert Burns' poem 'Cutty Sark', that malevolent witches cannot cross it.)

Some years ago, Janet was asked to travel to England to take action over the ill-thought-out behaviour of certain witches. She had the support of some very experienced Crafters in this and knew it was necessary both for the health of the Craft and for its public image; but she knew too that it would raise a storm, not only from the people concerned but even from some genuine witches who were well-intentioned but incompletely informed about what processes these people's actions would set in motion.

She did what was necessary, and when some of her experienced supporters saw her off on her boat-train from London, she admitted to a touch of anxiety about the mud which was already beginning to fly.

She was told: 'Don't worry too much. We've put up a fog for you.'

Janet took this to be metaphorical, but from the moment the boat sailed until it docked in Ireland, it was surrounded by thick fog, which cleared as soon as she landed.

The whole dispute is, fortunately, water long under the bridge; suffice it to say that Janet weathered the storm.

# XX   *Odd Ones Out*

Daniel Cohen of London has drawn our attention to an interesting, and hitherto unpublicized, case of multi-group working. It related to the arrest in 1981 of Peter Sutcliffe, the 'Yorkshire Ripper', for the brutal murder of thirteen women between 1975 and 1980, and concerns the work of Diana Scott, a fine poet living in Leeds, where most of the murders were committed. She gave Daniel permission to quote her for our book.

She was moved to write the 'Poem for Jacqueline Hill' (the Ripper's thirteenth and last victim)

> ... partly based on what other women had been saying and doing in their women's groups – this included various forms of magic, with various degrees of training ranging from almost none to well-trained.
>
> This poem, originally published anonymously, had very wide circulation – the full poem was distributed at a number of feminist events, and quite long sections appeared in *The Guardian*, the *Yorkshire Post* and elsewhere. It acted as a focus for women's energies, and this

may well have led to Sutcliffe's arrest (he had been questioned several times earlier, but to no effect).

This very moving poem is much too long to reproduce here, but it can be found on p. 273 of the anthology *Bread and Roses* (compiled by Diana Scott, Virago Press, 1982). It includes a passage in the name of the 'thirteen long shadows':

> May they draw the light from your eyes, Ripper
> May they draw the blood from your body, Ripper
> till all you are is in the deep shadow
> of your own hatred for us, Ripper,
> following you swift and pathless as a scream
> and you will kill no more:
> LET IT BE SO

Diana was very unsure about the 'curse' section; she did not like the idea of cursing but felt that it was a necessary expression of women's feelings. After discussing this with Daniel and others, she put in the line which fuelled the curse by his own hatred – 'That seemed the best solution, as it meant that the curse would lift if his hatred disappeared.'

Cursing, as we have made quite clear, is normally as dangerous to the curser as it is to the cursed, and Diana obviously knew this. But in these special circumstances, where she was expressing poetically the entirely justifiable anger of her fellow-women (and, one must add, of countless men), we feel that Daniel's advice was sound. It could be said that, in fact, the 'curse' was both a binding spell (see Chapter XIX) and an invocation of the Boomerang Effect (see Chapter IV), which would cease if and when Sutcliffe's hatred ceased.

It does seem that the wide circulation of the poem made it a focus of many people's energies; and this is a vivid example of the power of verse which we mentioned on p. 34.

From 1975 to 1978, Sutcliffe had managed to evade one of the largest police operations northern England had ever seen, but from then on the clues began to accumulate. He seemed to become clumsy; the last two women whom he attacked before Jacqueline Hill actually escaped. This change of behaviour was surprising after three years of successful silent cunning – and who is to say that the widespread magical working did not stimulate both the change and the fact that he was finally caught almost by chance?

If a malignant person is determined enough, magical working which fails to stop him immediately may nonetheless trigger him into destroying himself or may provide a small everyday seed which finally blossoms into his downfall.

On a much lighter note. Gerry from Vancouver tells us that some years ago, when he was a child, they moved to a new house. The youngsters of the family 'threw a spell' (his phrase). 'I'm not sure that we really knew what we were doing, but the gist of the spell was that if the new owners didn't love the house as much as we did, may they move quickly. The new owners lasted all of two months, and the next owners only one month. The third owners have lived there ever since.'

Children can indeed be powerful spell-workers; the three essentials of visualization, concentration and will-power come naturally to them. Their imaginative visualization can be so vivid that it competes with and overlaps mundane reality. Their concentration may sometimes be brief but while it lasts can be more absolute than most adults can achieve. And as for will-power – every parent is familiar with the intensity of a child's 'I want!'

We are talking here particularly about very young, pre-teenage children. By the time they reach their teens, rationalist education, the confusion of incoming data, and the growing realization that there are few simple answers will have worked to blunt the original childhood innocence, clarity and single-mindedness. This blunting may be temporarily offset by the arrival of puberty, because a pubertal girl or boy tends to be a psychic volcano – witness the frequency with which they feature in cases of poltergeist phenomena.

But to return to the very young. The general feeling in the Craft is that children should not take part in working Circles, as distinct from festivals, but that their natural sense of magic is to be encouraged and gently guided along constructive lines, since (like Gerry of Toronto) they'll be exercising it anyway.

In our *The Witches' God* (pp. 84–5) we suggested a little spell for children which we feel is a sound example of this. It involves telling them the story of Isis and Osiris and how the Ancient Egyptians saw the fertility of the Nile valley on which their lives depended. Millions of people in the world today are going hungry, and we have Self Aid, Band Aid, Comic Relief and so on to help them – so why not Magic Aid?

The child cuts out a piece of flannel in the shape of a man (in that context, of Osiris), keeps it damp on a plate and sows mustard-and-cress seeds on it. As they germinate and grow, he wishes that the hungry people of the world shall have more food.

Such spells are fun as well as sound teaching.

Parents can have quite a lot of fun themselves, using their imagination to devise suitable spells for their children. And as Michael Bentine points out (*The Door Marked Summer*, p. 36): 'Evil and negative forces abhor the sound of genuine laughter.... Hatred, in particular, instantly dissolves in the presence of a good old down-to-earth guffaw.'

Talking of laughter, here is an example of spell-working which appears, on the face of it, to break the rules about clear visualization by the whole group involved.

The family of one of our witches planned to emigrate from Ireland to Australia, and she asked us to work for them. They were waiting a little anxiously for the necessary Australian permission and looking for a buyer for their Irish house.

We had already worked on 'normal' magical lines on their behalf, when Janet decided on a little extra. In the relaxed atmosphere of a Circle after the ritual and other workings were over, she announced a game with a magical purpose. We all sat round a lit candle, and she started a story which we had to continue in rotation. We had to use the words 'light', 'fire' and 'beer' as often as possible but must not use the word 'and'. Whenever a narrator said 'and', the candle was blown out and re-lit, and the next person had to take up the story.

The storytelling became more and more bizarre and hilarious, and peppered with such things as 'Marks plus Spencer', and everybody wondering just what Janet had in mind. Finally, and quite unwittingly, somebody used the word 'Earth' – and Janet declared the game over and its power discharged.

She then explained. The words 'light' and 'fire' related to the positive aspects of the family's plans, 'beer' to the image of Australia, and 'Earth', quite simply, to their getting there successfully. Janet had kept all this clearly in mind and used the tension of our curiosity, and our laughter, to build up the power. When the key word came, she released it.

Within a week, the family's official permission came through, and they contracted the sale of their house for a rather better price than they had expected. Up till then the family had regarded the daughter's witchcraft as something of a harmless hobby, but now even the cynics among them (including a genius mathematician) admitted to second thoughts.

The moral of the storytelling spell is the same one that appears in many other fields: that once you have truly mastered the rules, you know just when and how to bend them.

Stewart was brought up a Christian Scientist – a religion with much undoubted success in psychic healing, though its identification of the material plane with illusion and evil we find totally unacceptable. But there is at least one story from that upbringing which he enjoys remembering and which seems to underline the fact that successful spell-working depends on clear visualization and total confidence.

There is a much-quoted passage in the works of Mary Baker Eddy, the religion's founder, which includes the phrase 'unfettered by human hypotheses'.

One little girl in a Christian Science family had a parrot which was moulting very badly. She told the family that she intended to work to cure it. Within a few days, the parrot's plumage began to restore itself. The parents asked her how she had worked.

'Easy,' she told them. 'I just knew it couldn't be unfeathered by human hypotheses.'

And one other story which might help spell-workers to keep a sense of proportion. There was a Christian Science practitioner (a whole-time, fee-charging healer) who was a friend of Stewart's parents. One day a woman came to him and told him that she had corrected all her faults and cured all her ailments except one – she still suffered from corns. Would he help her?

He looked at her thoughtfully for a moment and then said: 'Keep your corns, lady, and stay with us a little longer.'

Which became a family saying among the Farrars, quoted when anyone seemed a little short on reasonable self-criticism.

We might add in passing that there is one other aspect of Christian Science of which we do approve. It envisages God as 'our Father-Mother God'.

# XXI  *Tailpiece*

Some years ago, Janet was in a pub in East Anglia with a friend. It was the meeting-place of the local hunt, and they happened to be gathering there that morning.

On the wall behind the bar was a fox's head and brush. When the hunt had ridden off, the landlord reached up to the brush and turned it to point in the direction opposite to the way the hunt had gone.

Curious, Janet asked him why. He was a little embarrassed but was persuaded to explain. His father had been a keen huntsman and had put the head and brush there, but he himself disliked blood sports. He was understandably reluctant to quarrel with his best customers about it and knew they wouldn't listen anyway. But one day, on impulse, he had turned the brush round when the hunt took off, wishing vehemently that they would catch nothing. Since then, he had done it every time.

'I don't know why,' he finished diffidently, 'but it seems to work.'

We will not give away the name of the village or the pub – just in case he's still doing it. We wouldn't want to undermine his efforts.

# Appendix 1: *Planetary Hours*

| Hours from sunrise | Sunday | Monday | Tuesday | Wednesday | Thursday | Friday | Saturday |
|---|---|---|---|---|---|---|---|
| 1st | Sun | Moon | Mars | Mercury | Jupiter | Venus | Saturn |
| 2nd | Venus | Saturn | Sun | Moon | Mars | Mercury | Jupiter |
| 3rd | Mercury | Jupiter | Venus | Saturn | Sun | Moon | Mars |
| 4th | Moon | Mars | Mercury | Jupiter | Venus | Saturn | Sun |
| 5th | Saturn | Sun | Moon | Mars | Mercury | Jupiter | Venus |
| 6th | Jupiter | Venus | Saturn | Sun | Moon | Mars | Mercury |
| 7th | Mars | Mercury | Jupiter | Venus | Saturn | Sun | Moon |
| 8th | Sun | Moon | Mars | Mercury | Jupiter | Venus | Saturn |
| 9th | Venus | Saturn | Sun | Moon | Mars | Mercury | Jupiter |
| 10th | Mercury | Jupiter | Venus | Saturn | Sun | Moon | Mars |
| 11th | Moon | Mars | Mercury | Jupiter | Venus | Saturn | Sun |
| 12th | Saturn | Sun | Moon | Mars | Mercury | Jupiter | Venus |

| Hours from sunset | Sunday | Monday | Tuesday | Wednesday | Thursday | Friday | Saturday |
|---|---|---|---|---|---|---|---|
| 1st | Jupiter | Venus | Saturn | Sun | Moon | Mars | Mercury |
| 2nd | Mars | Mercury | Jupiter | Venus | Saturn | Sun | Moon |
| 3rd | Sun | Moon | Mars | Mercury | Jupiter | Venus | Saturn |
| 4th | Venus | Saturn | Sun | Moon | Mars | Mercury | Jupiter |
| 5th | Mercury | Jupiter | Venus | Saturn | Sun | Moon | Mars |
| 6th | Moon | Mars | Mercury | Jupiter | Venus | Saturn | Sun |
| 7th | Saturn | Sun | Moon | Mars | Mercury | Jupiter | Venus |
| 8th | Jupiter | Venus | Saturn | Sun | Moon | Mars | Mercury |
| 9th | Mars | Mercury | Jupiter | Venus | Saturn | Sun | Moon |
| 10th | Sun | Moon | Mars | Mercury | Jupiter | Venus | Saturn |
| 11th | Venus | Saturn | Sun | Moon | Mars | Mercury | Jupiter |
| 12th | Mercury | Jupiter | Venus | Saturn | Sun | Moon | Mars |

Ruling planets of the days of the week are as follows: Sunday, the Sun; Monday, the Moon; Tuesday, Mars; Wednesday, Mercury; Thursday, Jupiter; Friday, Venus; and Saturday, Saturn.

The first hour after sunrise belongs to the day's ruling planet. The following twelve hours are allocated to the other planets in the order Sun, Venus, Mercury, Moon, Saturn, Jupiter, Mars, in rotation, up to the sunset. The twelve hours from sunset to the next sunrise continue the sequence.

Of course, sunrise–sunset and sunset–sunrise are only exactly twelve hours each at the equinoxes. At other times, one can either use sixty-minute hours for as long as day or night lasts, but always starting with the traditional planet at sunrise or sunset; or one can divide each period by twelve and use these shorter or longer 'hours'.

The traditional sources differ on the subject or are unclear, so the only thing to do is to settle on the method which feels right to you, and stick to it.

# Appendix 2: *Planetary Squares*

| 4 | 9 | 2 |
|---|---|---|
| 3 | 5 | 7 |
| 8 | 1 | 6 |

SATURN

| 4 | 14 | 15 | 1 |
|----|----|----|----|
| 9 | 7 | 6 | 12 |
| 5 | 11 | 10 | 8 |
| 16 | 2 | 3 | 13 |

JUPITER

| 11 | 24 | 7 | 20 | 3 |
|----|----|----|----|----|
| 4 | 12 | 25 | 8 | 16 |
| 17 | 5 | 13 | 21 | 9 |
| 10 | 18 | 1 | 14 | 22 |
| 23 | 6 | 19 | 2 | 15 |

MARS

| 6 | 32 | 3 | 34 | 35 | 1 |
|---|----|---|----|----|---|
| 7 | 11` | 27 | 28 | 8 | 30 |
| 19 | 14 | 16 | 15 | 23 | 24 |
| 18 | 20 | 22 | 21 | 17 | 13 |
| 25 | 29 | 10 | 9 | 26 | 12 |
| 36 | 5 | 33 | 4 | 2 | 31 |

SUN

| 22 | 47 | 16 | 41 | 10 | 35 | 4 |
|----|----|----|----|----|----|---|
| 5 | 23 | 48 | 17 | 42 | 11 | 29 |
| 30 | 6 | 24 | 49 | 18 | 36 | 12 |
| 13 | 31 | 7 | 25 | 43 | 19 | 37 |
| 38 | 14 | 32 | 1 | 26 | 44 | 20 |
| 21 | 39 | 8 | 33 | 2 | 27 | 45 |
| 46 | 15 | 40 | 9 | 34 | 3 | 28 |

VENUS

| 8 | 58 | 59 | 5 | 4 | 62 | 63 | 1 |
|---|----|----|---|---|----|----|---|
| 49 | 15 | 14 | 52 | 53 | 11 | 10 | 56 |
| 41 | 23 | 22 | 44 | 45 | 19 | 18 | 48 |
| 32 | 34 | 35 | 29 | 28 | 38 | 39 | 25 |
| 40 | 26 | 27 | 37 | 36 | 30 | 31 | 33 |
| 17 | 47 | 46 | 20 | 21 | 43 | 42 | 24 |
| 9 | 55 | 54 | 12 | 13 | 51 | 50 | 16 |
| 64 | 2 | 3 | 61 | 60 | 6 | 7 | 57 |

MERCURY

| 37 | 78 | 29 | 70 | 21 | 62 | 13 | 54 | 5 |
| 6 | 38 | 79 | 30 | 71 | 22 | 63 | 14 | 46 |
| 47 | 7 | 39 | 80 | 31 | 72 | 23 | 55 | 15 |
| 16 | 48 | 8 | 40 | 81 | 32 | 64 | 24 | 56 |
| 57 | 17 | 49 | 9 | 41 | 73 | 33 | 65 | 25 |
| 26 | 58 | 18 | 50 | 1 | 42 | 74 | 34 | 66 |
| 67 | 27 | 59 | 10 | 51 | 2 | 43 | 75 | 35 |
| 36 | 68 | 19 | 60 | 11 | 52 | 3 | 44 | 76 |
| 77 | 28 | 69 | 20 | 61 | 12 | 53 | 4 | 45 |

## MOON

It will be noticed that, in each square, the numbers in each of the rows, horizontal or vertical, add up to the same total. These totals are: Saturn 15, Jupiter 34, Mars 65, Sun 111, Venus 175, Mercury 260 and Moon 369.

Users of Barrett's *Magus* should note that there is an error in his Venus square: the third number from the left in the second row should be 48, not 43, as the row-totals will confirm. This error has been repeated in various texts, including Israel Regardie's otherwise excellent *How to Make and Use Talismans*.

To turn a name into a planetary-square sigil, convert its letters to numbers according to this table:

| 1 | 2 | 3 | 4 | 5 | 6 | 7 | 8 | 9 |
|---|---|---|---|---|---|---|---|---|
| A | B | C | D | E | F | G | H | I |
| J | K | L | M | N | O | P | Q | R |
| S | T | U | V | W | X | Y | Z |   |

Then trace the name over the chosen square in a continuous line from number to number. Example: the name Regardie converts to the numbers 9, 5, 7, 1, 9, 4, 9, 5. On the square of the Sun, this would produce the sigil shown in Fig. 5.

You will notice that it is customary to start the sigil with a small circle and end it with a T-cross. (The actual squares, included here to clarify the process are of course omitted from the final sigil; see the one in Fig. 4 on p. 64.)

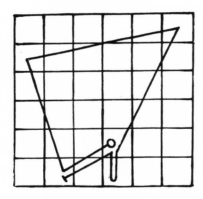

# Appendix 3:  *Magical Alphabets*

Alphabets, whether public or esoteric, have from ancient times been regarded as having a magical power of their own. By 'public' we mean the standard alphabet of any given language, such as Egyptian, Greek or Hebrew. By 'esoteric' we mean alphabets used as a private code by magicians or occult fraternities.

We give below the alphabets of both categories which will be most useful to spell-workers, in two ways. First, for their own use (especially with talismans) in particular styles of working – for example, Ogham for Celtic, Runes for Saxon, or Hebrew for Cabalistic. And second, for understanding other people's magical writings or artefacts which may come into their hands.

For one's own use, as Doreen Valiente puts it (*Witchcraft for Tomorrow*, p. 186): 'The significance of a magic alphabet is that it compels the writer to concentrate more deeply on what they are writing, because they have to express it in an unfamiliar and strange-looking script.'

We have not given the Egyptian alphabet, because its hieroglyphs run into so many hundreds – representing not only single sounds but syllables, disyllables and determinatives – that its magical use or understanding demands a lot of study, and even an outline of it would take up many pages. For those who are really interested, we recommend the standard work, Gardiner's *Egyptian Grammar*; or for a simple introduction, Wallis Budge's *Egyptian Language* or the Scotts' *Egyptian Hieroglyphs for Everyone* (see Bibliography for all these).

## PUBLIC ALPHABETS

### Hebrew
Of all the public alphabets, this is the most deliberately and specifically magical. Every letter has its own meaning and numerical value, and these are related to the system of the Cabala; the essential relationships and correspondences will be found in Crowley's *777*, and something of their Hebrew meanings in Isidore Kozminsky's *Numbers: Their Meaning and Magic*. A Hebrew name's sequence of letters would thus be a simple or complex formula of constituent meanings; much of the esoteric meaning of the Old Testament is hidden in the Cabalistic formulae of the names used.

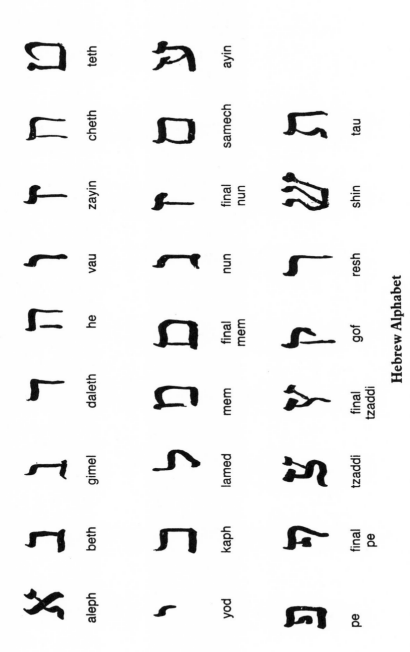

**Hebrew Alphabet**

| A α alpha | B β beta | Γ γ gamma | Δ δ delta | E ε epsilon | Z ζ zeta | H η eta | Θ θ theta |
| I ι iota | K κ kappa | Λ λ lamda | M μ mu | N ν nu | Ξ ξ xi | O ο omikron | Π π pi |
| P ρ rho | Σ σς sigma | T τ tau | Υ υ upsilon | Φ φ phi | X χ khi | Ψ ψ psi | Ω ω omega |

**Greek Alphabet**

## Greek

Greek lettering is, of course, useful for such things as talismans invoking a Greek deity, but you would be wise to look him or her up in a Greek dictionary first, as the accepted modern spelling often differs. Demeter, for example, is actually Demetra (Δήμητρα). And you need to know if an 'e' or an 'o' is long or short, since these have different letters. (This may sound pedantic, but a determination to 'get things right' is a healthy approach to spell-working.)

## Ogham Script

'Ogham' should be pronounced 'Oh-am'; it is named after the Irish Celtic god of wisdom and writing, Oghma (pronounced 'Oh-ma'), who is said to have invented it. Throughout most of their history, the Celts did not use writing; their wisdom and knowledge were preserved and handed on by word of mouth, by druids and bards who had long training in the method. Ogham script was a late development, found mostly on memorial and other stones; it was, as can be seen, ideally suited for engraving along the right-angled edge of a slab. *See* page 174.

## Runes

Runes were the first Germanic alphabet, which developed into slightly differing Scandinavian and Anglo-Saxon forms, with local variants. Originating about the third century AD, they were still in use in remote Swedish districts almost till our own times. They were always regarded as magical; the name itself comes from the Old Norse *run*, meaning 'whisper, secret counsel, mystery', and acquired the secondary meaning of a magical song, as in the Wiccan 'Witches' Rune'. Norse legend says they were magical signs first and only later came to be used for writing. They are often known as Futhorc or Futhark runes, from the first six letters of their traditional order. (Below, we have put them in ABC order for simplicity of reference.)

Before we list them, here is an invocation for use with a rune spell suggested by Michael Howard in his book *The Magic of the Runes*:

> Odin, upholder of the Sun and the ocean,
> Supporter of the Moon, All father!
> Possessor of arcane wisdom,
> Lord of the Faery Hosts,
> Wild Hunter of the Midwinter sky,
> Ruler of the Underworld and the crossroads,
> I —, invoke and call upon thee
> To aid me in the Great Work.
>
> At the time I seek [state your intention]
> with thy help and through the wisdom of
> the magical runes which are under thy protection.

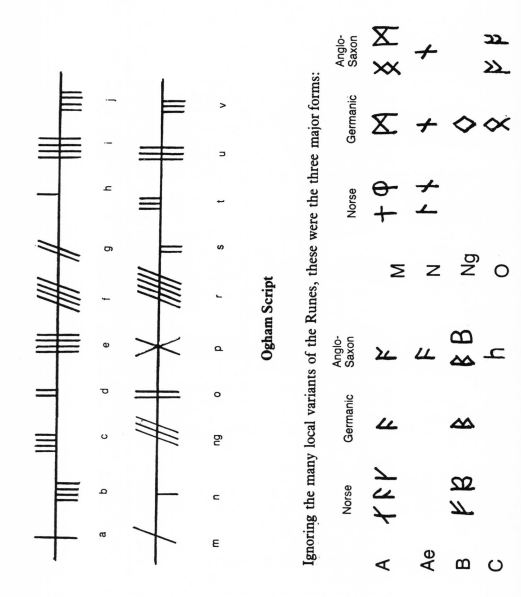

**Ogham Script**

Ignoring the many local variants of the Runes, these were the three major forms:

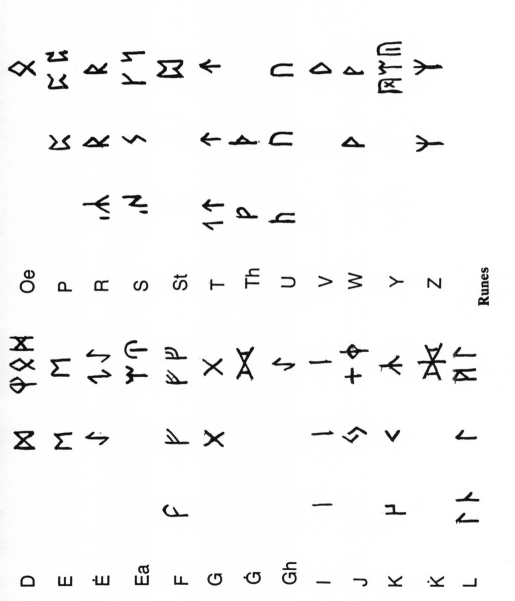

## ESOTERIC ALPHABETS

Several esoteric alphabets have been used by ceremonial magicians from the Middle Ages onwards, and adopted by witches. Of these, the Theban seems to be the most popular among contemporary witches – perhaps because it equates best to the English letters. The Celestial, Malachim, Passing the River and Magi scripts are based on Hebrew.

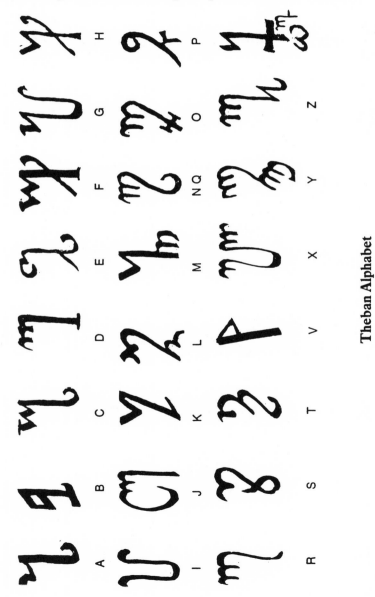

Theban Alphabet

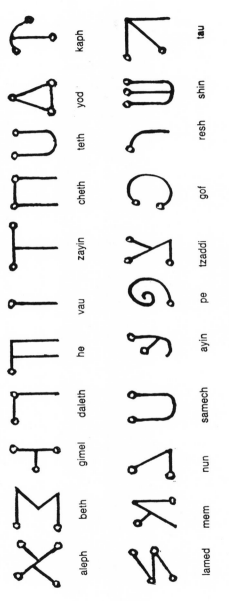

**Celestial Script**

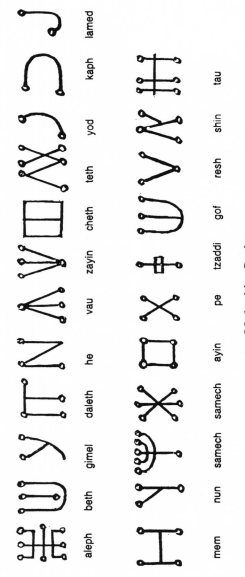

**Malachim Script**

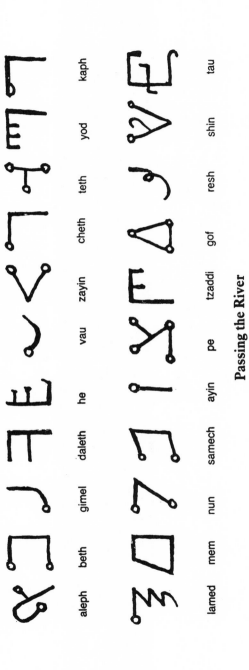

**Passing the River**

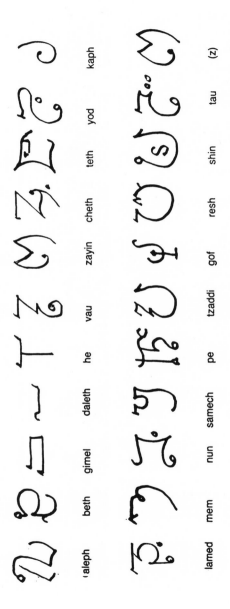

**Writing of the Magi**

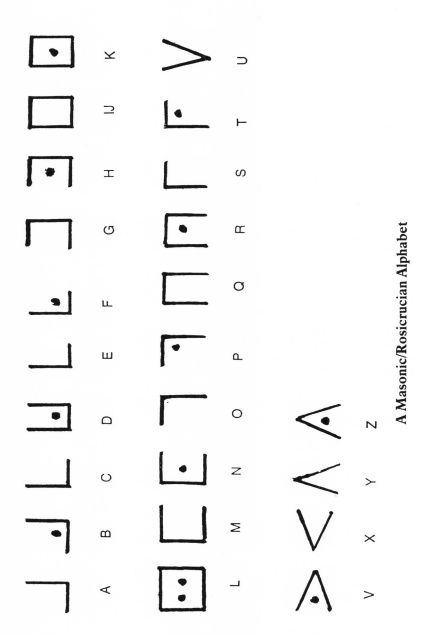

A Masonic/Rosicrucian Alphabet

# Appendix 4: *Some Suppliers*

Here is a selection of suppliers of items that can be useful for spell-working. It is not meant to be comprehensive, and no criticism is intended of those doubtless excellent suppliers who are not included. This list merely covers suppliers whom we have ourselves used and found satisfactory. We suggest you write to them for price lists.

Acca & Adda, BCM Akademia, London WC1N 3XX. Mail-order incenses and oils.

Anubis Books, 28 Bury Street, Heywood, Lancs.

Arcania, 17 Union Passage, Bath, Avon. Occult supplies, books, incenses and oils.

Craefte Supplies Showroom, 33 Oldridge Road, London SW12. Occult supplies, books, incenses and oils.

Mirror Magic, Sue Quatermass, 32 The Diplocks, Weston Road, Hailsham, East Sussex. Attractive occult mirrors.

Mysteries, 9 Monmouth Street, London WC2. Occult supplies, books, incenses and oils.

Occultique, 73 Kettering Road, Northampton NN1 4AW. Occult supplies, books, incenses and oils.

Prince Elric, 498 Bristol Road, Sellyoak, Birmingham B29 68D.

The Sorcerer's Apprentice, 1 The Crescent, Hyde Park Corner, Leeds LS6 2NW. Occult supplies, books, incenses and oils.

Temple of the Mother, 84–6 The Bayle, Folkestone, Kent CT20 1SJ.

# Glossary

AMULET: An object worn as a protective charm. *See* Chapter IX.

ATHAME (Pronounced 'a-thay-me'): A witch's personal ritual knife, black-handled. It is never used for actual cutting (the only traditional exception to this rule being a hand-fasting cake). Ritually interchangeable with the sword (q.v.).

CABALA, QABALAH, KABBALA: *See* Chapter VIII.

CENSER: One of the elemental tools, representing the Air element. *See also* Sword, Wand.

CHALICE, CUP: One of the elemental tools, representing the water element and the feminine principle.

COVENSTEAD: A coven's regular place of meeting – or sometimes the area from which its membership is drawn.

DEOSIL: Clockwise, sunwise. Cf. Widdershins.

ELEMENTAL: (1) A simple non-material entity of the nature of one of the elements (q.v.). (2) A thought-form deliberately or unconsciously set up by concentrated will-power and/or emotion, by an individual or a group.

ELEMENTS: Earth, Air, Fire, and Water – plus Spirit, which integrates them all.

EVOCATION: The summoning of a non-material entity of a lower order than oneself. Cf. Invocation.

FAMILIAR: (1) An animal kept by a witch for the psychic help it can give, particularly in early warning of negative influences, to which cats, dogs and horses (for example) are particularly sensitive. (2) Sometimes used to describe an elemental (q.v.) in sense (2) above.

FETCH: (1) 'The apparition, double, or wraith of a living person' (*Oxford English Dictionary*). (2) A projected astral body or thought-form deliberately sent out to make its presence known to a particular person. (3) A witch (usually male) who acts as the High Priestess's messenger or escort; sometimes called the Officer or Summoner.

FITH-FATH: Same as Poppet (q.v.)

GNOME: The traditional name for an Earth elemental.

GREAT RITE: The major Wiccan ritual of male-female polarity. *See* Chapter VII.

GRIMOIRE: A (usually medieval) book or 'grammar' of magical procedures.

HEXAGRAM: (1) A six-pointed star, its two triangles signifying the occult principle of 'As above, so below'. The same as the Star of David, but its occult use is older. (2) Any one of the sixty-four six-line figures of the I Ching, a Chinese system of divination also much used in the West.

HIGH PRIEST: (1) The male leader of a coven, working partner of the High Priestess who is its overall leader. (2) Any second- or third-degree male witch. (The difference is between a coven appointment and a personal rank.)

HIGH PRIESTESS: (1) The female leader of a coven, and also its overall leader. (2) Any second- or third-degree woman witch; see previous entry.

INVOCATION: The invitation of an entity of a higher order than oneself. Cf. Evocation.

MAIDEN: In a coven, the High Priestess's principal female assistant for ritual purposes, who may or may not be her deputy in leadership. In earlier times, Maiden sometimes meant what we now mean by High Priestess.

PENTACLE: One of the elemental tools, representing the Earth element. A metal disc engraved with symbols, it is the centrepiece of the Wiccan altar.

PENTAGRAM: A five-pointed star, the points representing Earth, Air, Fire and Water, and the topmost point representing Spirit. For 'white' working, it is displayed with a single point uppermost (with the sole exception of the Wiccan second-degree sigil). 'Black' workers tend to display it reversed, with two points uppermost.

POPPET: A doll representing a particular person, used in healing or binding spells.

SALAMANDER: The traditional name for a Fire elemental.

SEPHIRA (sing.), SEPHIROTH (pl.): The ten spheres of the Cabalistic Tree of Life. *See* Chapter VIII.

SIGIL (pronounced to rhyme with 'vigil'): An occult seal or sign, usually unique to an individual or entity.

SKYCLAD: The witches' word for 'ritually naked'.

SWORD: One of the elemental tools, representing the Fire element – or, in some traditions, the Air element – and the masculine principle.

SYLPH: The traditional name for an Air elemental.

TALISMAN: An object similar to an Amulet (q.v.) but designed for a specific purpose and usually for a specific individual. *See* Chapter IX.

TANTRA: An Eastern system of spiritual development through sexual energy. *See* p. 49.

TREE OF LIFE: *See* Chapter VIII.

UNDINE: The traditional name for a Water elemental.

WAND: One of the elemental tools, representing the Air element (*see also* Censer) or, in some traditions, the Fire element (*see also* Sword).

WHITE-HANDLED KNIFE: Used for any actual cutting or inscribing necessary within the Magic Circle; cf. Athame.

WIDDERSHINS: Anti-clockwise: cf. Deosil.

WITCH'S LADDER: A string of forty beads, or a cord with forty knots, used (as is a rosary) for concentrated repetition without the distraction of actual counting.

# Bibliography

Barrett, Francis – *The Magus* (originally published 1801; facsimile reprint Vance Harvey Publishing, Leicester, 1970)

Bentine, Michael – *The Door Marked Summer* (Granada, St Albans, 1981)

Bharati, Agehananda – *The Tantric Tradition* (Rider, London, 1965; paperback 1975)

Bhattacharyya, Benoytosh – *Gem Therapy* (Firma K.L. Mukhopadhyay, Calcutta, 1971)

Bloomfield, Frena – *The Occult World of Hong Kong* (Hong Kong Publishing Co, 1980)

Bourne, Lois – *Witch Amongst Us* (Satellite Books, London, 1979)

Brown, Raymond Lamont – *A Book of Witchcraft* (David & Charles, Newton Abbot, 1971)

Budge, Sir E.A. Wallis – *Egyptian Language* (Routledge & Kegan Paul, London, and Dover Publications, New York, reprint 1970). *Egyptian Magic* (Routledge & Kegan Paul, London and Boston, reprint 1972)

Burland, C.A. – *The Magical Arts: A Short History* (Arthur Barker, London, 1966)

Chetwynd, Tom – *A Dictionary of Symbols* (Granada, St Albans, 1982)

Crow, W.B. – *Precious Stones: Their Occult Power and Hidden Significance* (Aquarian Press, London, 1968). *The Arcana of Symbolism* (Aquarian Press, 1970)

Crowley, Aleister – *777 Revised* (Neptune Press, London, 1952). *Magick* (Routledge & Kegan Paul, London, 1973)

Crowther, Arnold and Patricia – *The Secrets of Ancient Witchcraft* (University Books Inc., Secaucus, NJ, 1974)

Crowther, Patricia – *Lid Off the Cauldron* (Frederick Muller, London, 1981)

Culpeper, Nicholas – *Culpeper's Complete Herbal* (original, seventeenth century; current reprint, Foulsham & Co, Slough, Bucks)

Deren, Maya – *Divine Horsemen* (Thames & Hudson, London, 1953; paperback under the title *The Voodoo Gods*, Granada, St Albans, 1975)

Donovan, Frank – *Never on a Broomstick* (George Allen & Unwin, London, 1973)

Farrar, Janet and Stewart – *Eight Sabbats for Witches* (Robert Hale, London, 1981; Phoenix Publishing, Custer, WA, 1988). *The Witches' Way* (Hale, 1984; Phoenix, 1988). *The Witches' Goddess: The Feminine Principle of Divinity* (Hale, 1987); Phoenix, 1988). *Life & Times of a Modern Witch* (Piatkus Books, London, 1987: paperback Headline Books, London, 1988; Phoenix, 1988). *The Witches' God: Lord of the Dance* (Hale, 1989; Phoenix, 1989)

Farrar, Stewart – *What Witches Do* (originally published 1971; 2nd edition

185

Phoenix Publishing, Custer, WA, 1983)

Fernie, William T. – *The Occult and Curative Power of Precious Stones* (Rudolf Steiner Publications, New York, 1973)

Frazer, Sir J.G. – *The Golden Bough* (1922 original; abridged edition Macmillan, London, paperback, 1974)

Gardiner, Sir Alan – *Egyptian Grammar* (3rd edition, Oxford University Press, London, 1957)

Gardner, Gerald B. – *High Magic's Aid* (Houghton, London, 1949). *Witchcraft Today* (Rider, London, 1954) *The Meaning of Witchcraft* (Aquarian Press, London, 1959)

Gregory, Lady – *Visions and Beliefs in the West of Ireland* (first published 1920; 2nd edition Colin Smythe, Gerrards Cross, hardback 1970, paperback 1976)

Grimble, Arthur – *Return to the Islands* (John Murray, London, 1957)

Heaps, William – *Birthstones and the Lore of Gemstones* (Angus & Robertson, London, 1969)

Hope, Murry – *Practical Techniques of Psychic Self-Defence* (Aquarian Press, Wellingborough, Northants, 1983)

Howard, Michael – *The Magic of the Runes* (Aquarian Press, Wellingborough, Northants, 1980)

Inwards, Richard – *Weather Lore* (Rider, London, 1950)

Janssen, Sally E. – *A Guide to the Practical Use of Incense* (2nd revised edition, Triad Library & Publishing Co, St Ives, NSW, Australia, 1972)

Johns, June – *King of the Witches: The World of Alex Sanders* (Peter Davies, London, 1969)

Kozminsky, Isidore – *Numbers: Their Meaning and Magic* (first published 1912; 2nd edition, Rider, London, 1972)

Kramer, Heinrich, and Sprenger, James – *Malleus Maleficarum*, trans. by Montague Summers (paperback Arrow Books, London, 1971)

Leland, Charles G. – *Aradia: the Gospel of the Witches*, introduced by Stewart Farrar (C.W. Daniel, London, 1974)

Maple, Eric – *The Magic of Perfume* (Aquarian Press, Wellingborough, Northants, 1973)

Martello, Dr Leo Louis – *Witchcraft: The Old Religion* (University Books, Secausus, NJ, undated)

Mathers, S. Lidell MacGregor (translator and editor) – *The Key of Solomon the King (Clavicula Salomonis)* (originally published 1888; Routledge & Kegan Paul, London, 1972)

Morrison, Sarah Lyddon – *The Modern Witch's Spellbook* (Citadel Press, Secausus, New Jersey, 1971)

Mumford, John – *Sexual Occultism* (Llewellyn Publications, St Paul, Minn., 1975; Compendium Pty, Victoria, Australia, 1977)

Murray, Dr Margaret – *The Witch-Cult in Western Europe* (Oxford University Press, London, 1921). *The God of the Witches* (first published 1931; paperback Daimon Press, Castle Hedingham, Essex, 1962)

Neal, James H. – *Jungle Magic* (Harrap, London, 1966; paperback

Foursquare, London, 1967)

O'Farrell, Padraic – *Superstitions of the Irish Country People* (Mercier Press, Dublin, 1978)

Quinn, D. Michael – *Early Mormonism and the Magic World View* (Signature Books, Salt Lake City, Utah, 1987)

Radford, Edwin and Mona A. – *Encyclopaedia of Superstitions*, edited and revised by Christina Hole (Hutchinson, London, 1961)

Regardie, Israel – *How to Make and Use Talismans* (2nd edition, paths to Inner Power series, Aquarian Press, London, 1981)

Robbins, Rossell Hope – *The Encyclopaedia of Witchcraft and Demonology* (Spring Books, London, New York, Sydney and Toronto, 1959)

St George, E.A. – *The Casebook of a Working Occultist* (Rigel Press, London, 1972)

Sanders, Maxine – *Maxine: the Witch Queen* (Star Books, London, 1976)

Scott, Diana (compiler) – *Bread and Roses* (Virago, London, 1982)

Scott, Joseph and Lenore – *Egyptian Hieroglyphs for Everyone* (Funk & Wagnalls, New York, 1968)

Sephrial – *The Kabala of Numbers* (Newcastle Publishing, Van Nuys, Calif., 1974)

Seton, Julia, M.D. – *Symbols of Numerology* (Newcastle Publishing, North Hollywood, Calif., 1984)

Shah, Idries – *The Secret Lore of Magic* (Citadel Press, New York, 1970)

Shuttle, Penelope, and Redgrove, Peter – *The Wise Wound: Menstruation and Everywoman* (Gollancz, London, 1987)

Skelton, Robert – *The Practice of Witchcraft Today* (Robert Hale, London, 1988)

Slater, Herman (ed.) – *A Book of Pagan Rituals* (Samuel Weiser, York Beach, Me, 1978; Robert Hale, London, 1988)

Sturzaker, James – *Gemstones and Their Occult Power* (Merlin Publications, London, 1977)

Tarostar – *The Witch's Spellcraft* (International Imports, Toluca Lake, Calif., 1986). *The Witch's Formulary and Spellbook* (Original Publications, New York, undated)

Valiente, Doreen – *Where Witchcraft Lives* (Aquarian Press, London, 1962). *An ABC of Witchcraft Past and Present* (Robert Hale, London, 1973). *Natural Magic* (Robert Hale, London, 1975). *Witchcraft for Tomorrow* (Robert Hale, London, 1978). *The Rebirth of Witchcraft* (Robert Hale, London, 1989)

Waters, Frank – *Book of the Hopi* (Ballantine Books, New York, 1969).

Wedeck, Harry E. – *A Treasury of Witchcraft* (Philosophical Library, New York, 1961; Vision Press, London, 1968)

Wilde, Lady – *Ancient Legends, Mystic Charms and Superstitions of Ireland* (originally published 1888; paperback reprint O'Gorman Ltd, Galway, 1971)

Worth, Valerie – *The Crone's Book of Words* (Llewellyn Publications, St Paul, Minn., 1971)

# Index